Knockouts

Odysseus returns

Knockouts

General Editor: Josie Levine

Cassette tapes with readings from the books, are available
   for the following:
The Marco File read by Robert Powell
Save The Last Dance For Me read by Valentine Dyall
Stranger than tomorrow read by Edward Petheridge
The Six read by Tony Robinson
The Six: Getting By read by Michael Burlington and Anthony Hyde
The Six: Turning Points read by David Goodland and Brian Hewlett
*A Northern Childhood: The Balaclava Story
   and other stories* read by George Layton
A Northern Childhood: The Fib and other stories read by George Layton
Long Journey Home read by Guy Gregory and Valerie Murray
Odysseus Returns read by Christian Rodska
The Robe of Blood read by Jill Balcon
The Bakerloo Flea read by Michael Rosen
You Can't Explain Everything read by Miriam Margolyes

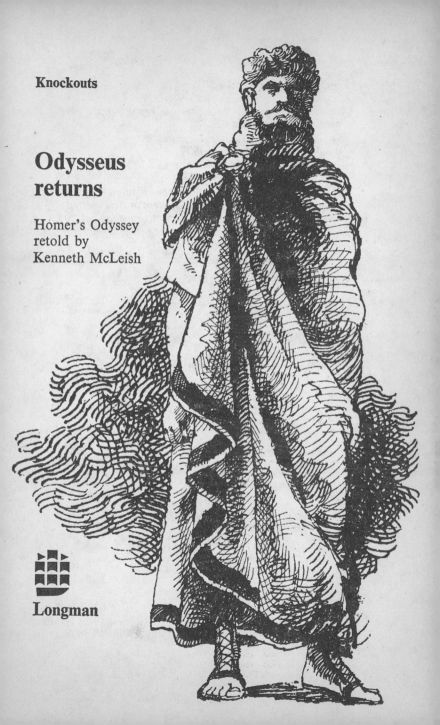

Knockouts

Odysseus
returns

Homer's Odyssey
retold by
Kenneth McLeish

Longman

Longman Group Limited
London
*Associated companies, branches and representatives
throughout the world.*

Text © Kenneth McLeish 1977
Illustrations © Longman Group Ltd 1977

First published 1977
Reprinted 1980

for Jeremy O. Nichols

ISBN 0 582 22219 2

Illustrations by Charles Front

Printed in England by Hazell Watson & Viney Ltd,
Aylesbury

Contents

Characters in the story

Mortals

Penelope.
Odysseus' wife.

Odysseus, King of Ithaka.
He has been away from home
nearly twenty years.
The first ten years
were spent helping the Greeks
to capture the city of Troy.
When Troy was captured,
Odysseus set off for home.
Many disasters and fights
have stopped him from reaching home.
Most people in Ithaka think he is dead.
Only his wife and son and a few servants
stay faithful to him.

Telemachos, the son
of Odysseus and Penelope.

Gods

Zeus, the king of the gods.

Athene, the goddess of wisdom.
She watches over the fortunes
of Odysseus and his family.
She often disguises herself as a mortal
in order to be able to appear to them
and talk with them.

Other mortals in the story

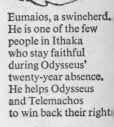

Eumaios, a swineherd.
He is one of the few
people in Ithaka
who stay faithful
during Odysseus'
twenty-year absence.
He helps Odysseus
and Telemachos
to win back their right

Antinoös, Eurymachos and their friends.
They are trying to persuade Penelope
that her husband is dead, and to convince her
that she should marry one of them.
Sometimes they are called by their names,
and sometimes they are called: the suitors.

King Alkinoös of Phaïakia.
He looks after Odysseus
during the last part of Odysseus'
journey home.

Menelaos and Helen,
king and queen of Sparta.
It is in their palace
that Telemachos hears
good news of his father.

Other gods in the story

Kalypso.
She is in love with Odysseus,
and, at the beginning of this story,
she has him trapped on her island.
By the will of the gods,
Odysseus escapes from her.

Poseidon, the god of the sea.

Hermes, the messenger of the gods.

The gods take action

The sun was hot, in a clear blue sky. In the harbour, boats dozed lazily at anchor. In the village old men sat in the shade, dreaming, while children played at their feet. It was like any other peaceful summer day.

But Prince Telemachos was angry. Tossing his cloak over one shoulder, he walked quickly from the great hall of the palace. In the court-yard the slaves were hard at work. The men were mixing wine, and carving meat for the evening feast. The women were sponging tables, and shaking out rugs and cushions from the great hall.

Telemachos looked at them with disgust. Another feast for those useless suitors! Another wasted day! he thought grimly. He turned and walked up the dusty road to the headland.

He soon reached the top, where the cliff hung sheer over the foaming sea below. Shading his eyes from the sun, he gazed out to sea. He'd come to the same place, and done the same thing, every day since he was a boy. And every day it was just the same. The sea was beautiful. The waves glittered in the sun. But it was empty. There were no sails; no ships, nothing, as far as the eye could see.

Telemachos stood for a while, then turned sadly away. He hitched his cloak round his shoulders, and started back for the palace.

Then all at once, out of nowhere, the sky turned inky black. Telemachos stopped, like a man struck blind. There was a deafening crack of thunder, sharp as a whiplash. A streak of lightning split the sky. Telamachos shut his eyes, waiting for the rain.

But none came. He opened his eyes, and stared in astonishment. The darkness had gone as quickly as it had come. The day was fine and hot again. And standing beside him was a stranger, someone he'd never seen before.

Where had he come from? A moment before, Telemachos had been alone on the headland. He wondered if the sun had affected his eyes. He rubbed them, and blinked. But when he opened them again, the stranger was still there. He was taller than ordinary men. His face was calm and still, without expression. His eyes were set deep in his head, and dark like the pools in a mountain stream. Telemachos has seen no one like him before.

The Prince stepped forward, and shook the stranger's hand.

'My friend,' he said. 'Whoever you are, and wherever you come from, I welcome you here in Ithaka. My kingdom is small, but we welcome every visitor, from land or sea. Come back with me to the palace. When you've eaten and drunk, you can tell us what brought you here.'

The stranger smiled, and bowed gravely. 'Thank you,' he said, in a quiet voice.

Telemachos led him down the road back to the palace. Inside, he propped the stranger's spear against a pillar, and led him to a chair with a lion-skin rug thrown over it. A slave brought water in a golden jug for them to wash their hands. Another slave put a table beside them, with bread and meat and fruit. The steward served wine in golden cups.

When they'd eaten all they wanted, Telemachos filled the stranger's cup with fresh wine.

'Now, my friend,' he said, 'tell me your news. Who are you? What brings you to Ithaka?'

'My lord Telemachos. . . ' the stranger began. But before he could go on, there was a great noise from outside. A gang of rowdy youths strolled into the great hall, whistling and shouting. They were princes from the great houses round about. They were well-dressed, but insolent. They sat down, and called roughly to the slaves to bring food and wine. The hall filled with the noise of laughter, talk, dirty jokes, and dogs barking as they snapped at titbits their masters tossed them.

Telemachos blushed.

'My friend,' he said to the stranger, 'I'm sorry. This is no way to welcome a guest. These are my mother's suitors.[1] They stroll in here like that every day. You'd think they owned the place. They do as they please, and no one can stop them.'

'You surprise me,' said the stranger, in a quiet voice. 'I thought this was the palace of a great king, not a club for rowdy youths.'

'It used to be. Once this was the palace of King Odysseus and his Queen, Penelope.'

'Once? Where's Odysseus now? Why do these young men flock here, like crows feasting on a rich carcass?'

'My father has been away for twenty years. He set sail for Troy, and no one here has seen him since.'

[1] suitor: a man who asks for a woman's hand in marriage.

'For Troy? But the war with Troy ended ten years ago.'

'My father still hasn't come home. These suitors say he must be dead; that his bones lie under the sea, or they are buried in some foreign land. They say it's time for my mother Penelope to marry again. Until she chooses one of them, they say they'll come here every day. Every day will be a feast-day, until nothing is left of my father's wealth.'

'Can't you do anything to stop them?'

'My friend, I'm brave, but not stupid. How could one man send the whole gang packing? No, I must bite my lip, and put up with their insults in silence.'

The stranger stood up. He was taller and more powerful than ordinary men. His deep, dark eyes flashed with sudden fire. 'You're wrong, Telemachos!' he said. 'The time has come for you to show whose son you are. The gods send you this message. Go to the harbour and set sail for Sparta. King Menelaos and Queen Helen will welcome you. They have news of your father.'

'News? What news?'

'Only the gods know that. If Odysseus is alive, and coming home, you can put up with these suitors till he arrives. But if he's dead, you must bury him and tell your mother to marry again. You're a grown man. Act like Odysseus' son!'

Telemachos looked into the stranger's eyes, and knew that he must obey.

'These orders come from the gods,' he said, 'and I must follow them.'

'And quickly, too!' said the stranger. 'Go to the harbour tomorrow. A boat will be waiting, stocked with food and wine, and with the best crew in Ithaka. And now I must go, too. The gods' message is delivered.'

'Wait!' cried Telemachos. But he was too late. There was a crash of thunder, and the stranger vanished before his eyes, soaring like a bird through the smoke-hole in the roof. Telemachos felt goose-pimples all over his body. He'd been talking to no ordinary mortal. The stranger was one of the gods themselves.

He turned back to the suitors. They were drunk, and full of noise. They were stamping their feet, and hammering the tables with their wine-cups.

'Penelope! Penelope!' they chanted. 'We want Penelope!'

Angrily Telemachos stood up.

'Be quiet!' he shouted. 'This is no way to court a queen. My mother will stay where she is, in the women's part of the palace. Isn't it enough that you guzzle my father's food and wine while he's not at home to prevent it?'

'Listen to him!' sneered Antinoös, the suitors' leader. 'Big talk, from a pretty little prince!'

He swaggered over to Telemachos, and looked at him mockingly. 'Big talk!' he said, his thumbs hooked in his belt. 'Suppose we don't sit down? Who's going to make us? You?'

'Don't be a fool, Antinoös,' answered Telemachos quietly. 'There's nothing I'd like better than a fight. But the gods have taken a hand. If they decide that my father is dead, and one of you is to marry my mother, I'll accept their decision. But until then, I'm master in this house, and I'll make you mind your manners.'

Antinoös looked furious. But he went slowly back to his place and sat down.

'Bring more wine!' he shouted. 'Bring out Odysseus's best! If the gods are going to make us wait, at least we'll enjoy ourselves while we do it!'

The other suitors roared agreement. They held out their cups for wine, and ordered the minstrel Phemios to play and sing for them.

The party went on all day and into the night. But Telemachos sat quietly in a corner by himself. He was turning over in his mind the message the gods had sent him, and making his plans for the following day.

The council

Next morning at dawn, Telemachos was up and dressed. He slung his sword from his shoulder, put on his sandals, and hurried out into the courtyard. His slaves were waiting.

'Go out into Ithaka, and call all the people to a council. They must come at once to the meeting-place. Let no man refuse to come.'

The messengers hurried away. Quickly the men of Ithaka began to gather. A council was only called when something really important had to be decided.

When everyone had arrived, Telemachos walked from his palace to the meeting-place. He was carrying a bronze spear, and two hunting-dogs trotted beside him. He looked as tall and as handsome as one of the gods themselves.

He sat down, and the council began. The first man to speak was Aigyptios. He was an old man, a friend of Telemachos' grandfather. Two of his sons were farmers at home, and another had been killed at Troy. The fourth was Eurynomos, one of the insolent young men who were Queen Penelope's suitors.

'People of Ithaka,' said Aigyptios, 'this is an important moment. There hasn't been a meeting of the people for twenty years – not since King Odysseus sailed for Troy. What is it? What business is so important that every man in Ithaka is called to discuss it? Who is it who sent for us?'

At once Telemachos got up, and took the speaker's place.

'I sent for you,' he said. 'My business is private, not public. But I want to speak out now, in front of all the men of Ithaka.'

There was a murmur of surprise. Some of the suitors sniggered. But the older men listened quietly, and Telemachos went on.

'You're all here, fathers and sons together. Some of you are my mother's suitors. I speak to you suitors, first. Every day you insult our palace, and feast at my father's expense. I pray to Zeus that one day Odysseus will come home, and pay you as you deserve. As for the rest of you, you are their fathers, and you should be ashamed as well. Marry your sons to women their own age. Tell them to stop courting Penelope. She's old enough to be their mother. She may be rich, and she may be a queen – but that's no reason for them to pester her, like hunting-dogs snapping at a cornered deer. She's married already, yet you let your sons insult her and her husband. Shame on them! And shame on you, for allowing it!'

When he finished, there was silence. No one had spoken so bluntly in Ithaka for years. The old men felt ashamed, and sorry for Telemachos. But the young suitors laughed, and sneered at him. Antinoös, their leader, swaggered to the speaker's place to answer him.

'Proud words!' he said scornfully. 'The puppy's beginning to pull at the leash at last!'

The suitors laughed rudely, and he went on: 'You're a fool, Telemachos, trying to put the blame on us. Your mother's to blame, not us.'

'My mother?' said Telemachos. 'What do you mean?'

'For the first four years she kept us at bay. Four years! She promised to make up her mind which of us to marry . . . soon. Always *soon*, never *now*. When our patience wore out, she tried another trick. She began to weave a beautiful robe. "For Laertes, Odysseus' father," she said. "To wrap him in when he's buried. As soon as it's finished, I'll choose a husband." Like fools, we believed her. After two years of it, one of her maids gave the secret away. The queen used to weave all day, but every night she had torches brought in, and unravelled it again. One night we caught her. She had no choice then. She had to finish it.'

'Well?'

'Well? *Well?* Of course it's not well! The robe's finished, and now she must choose one of us. Don't blame us for eating and drinking at Odysseus's expense. It's Penelope's fault, not ours.'

'Bold words,' said Telemachos. 'But you're in the wrong, and you won't get out as easily as that. I'm sailing to Sparta today, to visit Menelaos and get news of my father. When Odysseus returns, you'll wish you'd never been born.'

There was another stir. The suitors looked at each other in surprise. Telemachos had grown up! He'd changed since yesterday. Suddenly he was sailing to Sparta to get news of his father. He was getting too cock-sure. It was time he was stopped.

From up above, the gods saw how the council was going. Swiftly Zeus gave his orders. 'Athene, disguise yourself as a mortal.

Go round Ithaka quickly, and gather a ship and a crew for Telemachos. I'll give that council something to distract them, something to think about!'

At once Athene flew down to Ithaka. Disguising herself as Mentor, Telamachos' adviser, she chose the fastest ship in the harbour, and filled it with food for the journey. Then she went round collecting a crew. She collected the best and most skilful sailors she could find. They were eager to help: Mentor was a highly respected man in Ithaka.

Meanwhile Zeus kept the council busy. He sent two eagles down from Olympos. They banked and wheeled in the sun above the meeting-place, casting dark shadows on the council down below.

'Look!' called out Aigyptios. 'Sacred eagles! The gods are sending us an omen!'

Everyone gazed up at the eagles, shading their eyes against the sun.

For a moment the birds flew together in formation. Then, as they came over the very centre of the council, they began to fight. Wings flapped, beaks lunged, talons tore. Feathers and drops of blood fell to the ground. When they touched the earth they flared up like burning pitch, and vanished.

The eagles fought for about half a minute, tearing at each other's cheeks and necks. Then they swooped away eastwards, into the sun, and disappeared.

There was panic in the council. An omen! A fearful omen, from Zeus himself! What did it mean? Everyone looked at old Aigyptios. He was famous for his knowledge of birds. No one in Ithaka knew more about omens and prophecies.

Aigyptios stood up, and walked slowly to the speaker's place.

'Men of Ithaka,' he said, 'and you suitors in particular, listen to me. Those birds are a warning. Odysseus is coming home. The gods are helping him. Just as those eagles fought, so men will fight in Ithaka. When Odysseus returns, there will be war. Take my advice, and go home. Leave Penelope alone, or you'll suffer for it.'

Antinoös leapt up, and jostled Aigyptios out of the speaker's place.

'You grey-bearded old fool!' he shouted furiously. 'Go home and tell omens to your grandchildren! Stop *them* getting into mischief! No one here's afraid of you. No one here takes any notice of a pair of stupid birds!'

The suitors roared with approval. The older men shook their heads. They agreed with Aigyptios. Trouble was coming.

In the midst of the arguing, Athene went quietly up to Telemachos. She was still disguised as Mentor.

'Go now, Prince Telemachos. Your ship is waiting in the harbour.'

Telemachos looked into her eyes. He remembered them from the stranger of yesterday. Without a word, he got up and left the council. No one noticed him as he hurried off towards the harbour.

Athene stepped forward now.

'It's Mentor!' people said. 'Be quiet! Be quiet, and let Mentor speak!'

Athene waited for silence. Then she said, in Mentor's voice: 'Men of Ithaka, this council is getting nowhere. We've all seen an omen from Zeus. We've all heard Aigyptios explain it. Some of us believe him, and some don't. What's the use of arguing? Go home and think about what you've seen and heard today. That's my advice. Go home!'

The council broke up into ragged groups. Everyone went his own way. The old men shook their heads, and walked home in twos and threes.

'Trouble is coming,' they told each other. 'Trouble is coming, and Zeus has sent us a warning.'

The suitors swaggered off towards Odysseus' palace.

'Time for another feast!' they said. 'And as for Telemachos – he may set sail for Sparta, but he won't come back safely. We'll lay a trap for him – a fast ship, in hiding round a headland. Everyone will think his ship crashed on the rocks, and he was drowned.'

As they strolled into the palace courtyard, they laid their plots. They thought everything was safe. They thought they knew just what to do. But Athene knew what was in their minds.

She hurried to the harbour. There she gave Telemachos and his crew a following wind. The sail filled, and they were blown well out to sea, well on their way to Sparta.

Athene

All day and all night Telemachos and his crew sailed on. The sail gusted in the wind, and the dark blue water hissed along the keel of the boat.

At dawn they reached Pylos. King Nestor welcomed them, and gave Telemachos a fast chariot, and a pair of jet-black horses, to continue his journey by land. He sent his son with him, to act as guide.

'Will you come with us, Mentor?' Telemachos asked Athene.

'No. I've plenty to do in Ithaka. I'll see the ship back safely. You're a man now, Telemachos. You can look after yourself.'

Telemachos thanked him. He knew he'd see the goddess again. Then he climbed into the chariot beside King Nestor's son, and they galloped off down the road to Sparta.

By dusk, when roads are dark and dangerous, they had reached the palace of King Diokles. He was another friend of Odysseus from Trojan days. Like Nestor, he welcomed Telemachos for his father's sake, and gave him food and shelter for the night. Next morning, the travellers set out again. Soon they left the highlands, and came down into yellow corn-meadows, ripe and rippling in the summer sun.

All day their horses galloped tirelessly over the plains. As night fell they came to Sparta. The dust track turned into a magnificent paved road, leading to King Menelaos' palace.

King Menelaos' slaves welcomed them royally, for all travellers are protected by Zeus himself. They unyoked the sweating horses, and led them to the stables. They rubbed the horses down, and gave them a feed of oats and barley. Then, after they had leaned the chariot up against the palace wall, Telemachos and Nestor's son went in through the royal gate.

Telemachos had seen nothing like Menelaos' palace in his life. The pillared hall soared high above him, like the palace of the Sun himself. Each stone in the wall stood high as a man, and lay so snugly against the next that not even the thinnest sword-blade could pass between them.

Slaves filled baths of polished oak, and washed the dust and tiredness from the travellers. They rubbed them with scented oil, and dressed them in tunics and cloaks of purple wool. Then they led them to the great hall, where thrones were set up for them beside Menelaos himself.

A maid brought water for them to rinse their hands. Then she set a table beside them. The slaves brought bread and meat, and served them wine in golden cups. King Menelaos invited them to eat and drink.

'Welcome to Sparta, my friends,' he said. 'All travellers are welcome here. When you've eaten, you can tell us your business.'

As the young men ate, Queen Helen came down from the women's part of the palace. Her maids hurried to her side. One set out a comfortable chair, another covered it with a soft woollen rug, and a third brought in a work-basket of Egyptian silver. It was covered with small carvings, and topped with a rim of gold. Inside was fine-spun yarn,[1] and a spindle[2] wound with deep blue wool.

Queen Helen sat down, and began to spin. But her eyes never left the visitors. At last she

[1] yarn: thread made specially for weaving or spinning material.
[2] spindle: a holder shaped like a needle for the wool used in spinning or weaving.

laid down the spindle, and spoke to Menelaos.

'My lord, have we heard yet who these young men are? One is surely the son of King Nestor of Pylos. And the other! I'm amazed. He must be related to Odysseus himself. Twenty years ago, when the Greeks came to Troy to fetch me home, Odysseus looked just like him – the same hair, the same eyes, the same handsome face and noble bearing. Surely this young man is Telemachos, who was just a babe in arms when his father left for Troy.'

'My lady,' said Nestor's son, 'your guess is right. I'm the son of Nestor, King of Pylos. And this is Telemachos, Prince of Ithaka, the only son of Odysseus and Queen Penelope.'

'I thought so, too,' said Menelaos. 'I was waiting till you'd eaten, to ask you myself. Telemachos, your father was one of the bravest Greeks at Troy. I remember how we sat inside the Wooden Horse, while the Trojans lugged it into the city. It lurched and bumped over the stones. The hollow belly boomed and echoed. Every man there was afraid it would topple over, and spew us out in front of our enemies. Only Odysseus stayed calm. He prayed to Athene for help. His prayer and his example saved us, and helped us capture Troy.'

'I remember too,' said Helen, 'another time,

34

when the Greeks wanted to spy inside the city. Odysseus put on beggar's clothes, and flogged himself with his own hands, until his back was covered in raw wounds from the whip. Then he came whining and begging for bread in the city. No one thought such a starving beggar could be a prince of Greece. Only I saw through his disguise. But he made me swear to keep his secret, until he found out what he wanted, and left the city.'

'That's the sort of man he was,' said Menelaos. 'No one in the Greek army was braver or cleverer than Odysseus.'

Telemachos has been a tiny baby when his father had left Ithaka. He couldn't remember him at all. But now, when he heard him praised like this, he was filled with emotion. He put down his wine-cup, and covered his eyes with his hand. He was ashamed of the tears that filled them.

'But no more memories,' said Helen gently, noticing his distress.. 'You're welcome, Telemachos, worthy son of a noble father. What is it that brings you here to Sparta?'

'My lady,' began Telemachos. His voice was husky with emotion. 'If only the men of Ithaka remembered Odysseus as well as you do! There's a pack of suitors in his palace even now, fighting over my mother like dogs over a bone. They slaughter our animals, drink our wine, insult our guests. Menelaos, the gods say you have news of Odysseus. Please tell me where he is.'

Menelaos was red with anger.

'So!' he said. 'So all the cowards in Ithaka fancy their leader's bed? It's as if a deer left her fawns asleep in a lion's den, while she went foraging. Back comes the lion, and that's the end of them. That's how Odysseus will come home – like a lion on a pack of helpless fawns!'

'Then he *is* alive?' said Telemachos eagerly. 'You know that he's alive?'

'I know he's alive, and that he'll return. But I don't know where he is. He's marooned on a floating island, the home of the sea-nymph Kalypso. It travels over the sea, wherever the current takes it. Odysseus is trapped there. He can't escape, unless the gods help him.'

'Athene will help,' said Telemachos. 'She sent me here for this news. She'll help Odysseus to escape.'

'Then you've got what you came for,' said Menelaos. 'Now you must stay as my guest, and rest before you travel home. Slaves! Bring wine for Lord Odysseus' son!'

So Telemachos and his friend, the Prince of Pylos, were entertained in Menelaos' palace. There, they heard all about Odysseus' adventures in Troy, and of the long journey home of Menelaos and Helen, after the city was captured. All Menelaos' people came to see Telemachos, and the talk and feasting lasted many days.

Meanwhile, in Ithaka, the suitors were amusing themselves as usual, in the courtyard of Odysseus's palace. They were playing quoits,[1] and throwing the javelin. Only Antinoös and Eurymachos, their leaders, sat apart. Hovering overhead, unseen, Athene listened to their conversation.

'Telemachos has been gone a long time.'
'He'll be back soon enough.'
'Very soon. We must get the trap ready.'
'Is the ship waiting?'
'In the harbour, ready when we give the word. That brat won't ever see Ithaka again.'

Upstairs in the women's part of the palace, Penelope had also overheard their plot. She began to weep, and her maids could not comfort her.

'My husband, dead – and now my son's to

[1] quoits: a game in which each player has to throw an iron ring round a stick stuck in the ground.

die as well! How can I protect him? He's all I have, my only shield against these suitors! O Athene, if only you were nearby, and could hear my prayer!'

Athene heard, and acted. She made a moving image of flesh and blood just like Penelope's favourite maidservant. This image glided through the wall, and stood at the end of Penelope's bed. The Queen lay there, sobbing.

'Be still, mistress,' said the image gently. 'Your son isn't doomed. Your husband's safe, and he'll be home soon. The gods are watching and have promised to help.'

'Oh my friend,' said Penelope eagerly. 'My husband – alive? Where is he? Can you tell me that?'

'I can only tell you the words Athene has taught me. Now sleep, my child. The gods are watching.'

With these words, the image slipped through the crack in the door, and disappeared. Penelope felt her eyes closing. She was soon deep in a healing sleep.

Athene soared up to Olympus. She went straight to her father, Zeus.

'Sir,' she said, 'I've done all I can, now. Telemachos has had the news he went for, and

Penelope has been given new hope. But Odysseus is still trapped on Kalypso's floating island. That's his punishment for making your brother Poseidon angry. I can do nothing for him. But won't you take pity on him? Won't you change Poseidon's mind, and set Odysseus free?'

'Athene, you are right,' answered Zeus, lord of gods and men. 'Twenty years, to mortals, is a long time. Now I'll set Odysseus free.'

He called to Hermes, the winged messenger.

'Go down to Kalypso's floating island, and tell her that her love-affair is over. Odysseus must be set free. The day has come for his return.'

Poseidon is angry

Hermes flew down from Olympus. Like a seagull, swooping and dipping over the sea, he made his way to Kalypso's island. Kalypso was sitting at her loom, weaving. She recognised Hermes at once.

'Come in, and welcome,' she said. 'It's not often that the other gods come here to visit me. Sit down, and eat after your journey.'

She laid a rug over a polished wooden chair. Hermes sat down, and a slave brought water to rinse his hands. Another slave brought a table, and placed on it some of the gods' favourite food and drink – ambrosia and red nectar.

When he'd eaten and drunk, Hermes gave Kalypso the message from Zeus.

'Zeus, king of gods and men, has sent me to tell you this. Odysseus made Poseidon angry, and he's been punished. But now it's time for his punishment to end. He's to set out for Ithaka. No god or man will help him on his way. He must use all his strength and cunning.

40

After twenty days he'll reach Phaiakia. King Alkinoös will lend him a ship, and see him safely home. That's Zeus' message, and it must be obeyed at once.'

Kalypso was very angry.

'So that's it!' she said. 'You gods are all the same! Whenever a goddess falls in love with a mortal, you separate them! When Dawn loved Orion, you weren't satisfied until he died for it. When Demeter loved Iasion, Zeus sent a thunderbolt to kill him. Now I love Odysseus – and you want to tear him away from me. Is there no end to Zeus' jealousy?'

'Be careful. This island floats, far out of sight of land. But Zeus can still hear you. If you disobey, he'll punish you.'

Kalypso sighed.

'All right,' she said. 'Go back and tell him I'll obey.'

Hermes left the island, and flew back to Olympus. Kalypso went to find Odysseus. He was sitting on the shore, tossing pebbles into the sea. His heart was sad as he thought of his home in Ithaka, and the wife he thought he would never see again.

'Odysseus,' said Kalypso, 'your suffering is over. The gods have sent word. You're to leave the island at once.' As she spoke, tears ran down her cheeks. When Odysseus left, she'd be alone again.

Odysseus jumped angrily to his feet. 'Leave the island? How *can* I leave the island? There are no ships, no crews. Do you want me to swim, and drown? Is this another trick the gods are playing on me?'

'No, it's not a trick. You must build a raft. I'll help you. Start tomorrow. Let tonight be our last night of love together.'

She took Odysseus back to the cave. They feasted. He ate meat and bread, and drank sweet wine – the sort of food mortals enjoy. Kalypso ate ambrosia and drank the nectar of the gods. When they'd finished, they went to bed, and spent their last night together in each other's arms.

Next morning at dawn, Odysseus got up, and put his tunic and cloak on. Kalypso dressed in her shimmering, silvery robe. They ate their breakfast, and then began to plan for Odysseus' journey home.

Kalypso first gave him a huge, bronze axe, and a knife of polished metal. She took him to the far end of the island, where tall trees grew – alders, poplars and firs. They were old and dry, and would float on the roughest sea.

Kalypso left Odysseus there, and he set to

work. He cut down twenty trees, and trimmed their branches with the knife. He drilled holes in them, and fitted them across one another, to make a sturdy raft. He built sides for the raft out of wickerwork. This would keep the spray out. Then he made a mast and steering-oar out of polished oak.

Meanwhile Kalypso wove cloth for the sail. When it was ready, Odysseus plaited ropes, and fastened it to the mast. He made some oars, and finally he put a large stone in the raft, fastened to a rope, to act as the anchor.

The raft took four days to build. On the fifth day, he rolled it down on rollers into the calm sea. Kalypso brought food and water, and skins of wine. She bathed Odysseus, and dressed him in fine new clothes.

At last everything was ready. Odysseus kissed her goodbye, climbed onto the raft, and spread the sail. The wind was fresh, and soon he was carried far out to sea. Kalypso watched until she couldn't see him any more. Then she went back to her lonely cave, weeping quietly.

For seventeen days Odysseus sailed on, taking his course from the stars. In particular, he watched Orion. He had been a mortal once, too, and had once loved a goddess. But he had died for it. Now he was a star in the night sky, a guide to travellers all over the world.

On the eighteenth day, Odysseus saw land ahead. Phaiakia. This was the home of King Alkinoös, who would give him shelter, and see him safely home. Eagerly he spread his sail, and began rowing as well, to get there faster.

But now Poseidon, god of the sea, noticed him for the first time. He had been travelling far away, and had only just returned.

Poseidon was furious.

'So!' he said. 'I've only to turn my back, and the gods set Odysseus free! Another day, and he'll reach Phaiakia. Well, it's Zeus' will, and I can't prevent it. But I can make his journey a difficult one – and I will!'

He called the storm-clouds together, and began stirring up the sea with his powerful trident.[1] He brought winds from all sides, and covered land and sea with a thick, black storm. Rain fell; the wind howled; the waves rushed high as mountains.

Odysseus looked at the storm, and was filled with despair.

'Now what can I do?' he thought. 'So near safety – and now doomed! How can the gods help me now?'

As if in answer, Athene came down, dis-

[1] trident: a spear with three points.

guised as a seagull. She perched on the raft's side, her feathers fluttering in the wind.

'Odysseus!' she said. 'Save yourself! Poseidon means to sink this raft, and anything on it. Throw away those clothes, and dive naked into the sea. Take this veil, and wrap it round your waist. It will help you to reach land. When you're safe on shore, throw it out to sea again. Be brave, Odysseus! You'll need all your strength.'

Athene flew off into the storm. Odysseus looked at the mountainous waves in despair. How could he hope to survive, in a sea like that?

But the goddess had spoken, and given her orders. He stripped off his clothes, and fastened the veil round his waist. Then he waited till the raft rose high on the crest of a wave, and dived into the foaming sea.

He was just in time. The winds and waves picked up the raft, like puppies playing with a ball of wool. They tossed it about, and smashed it to pieces. Odysseus was left alone and naked in the stormy sea.

He swam for a day and a night. His arms were like lead weights, and his body so cold he couldn't feel it. At last he could swim no further. 'I've no strength left,' he thought.

'Whether I drown or survive, I can't swim another stroke.'

Athene had been watching. Zeus had forbidden any of the gods to help Odysseus. But she saw, coming up behind him, a huge wave. And just ahead of him was the rocky coast of Phaiakia.

The wave picked Odysseus up, and threw him at the land. He would have been smashed to pieces, if he hadn't had the sense to grab a huge rock, and cling on as the water surged over him. The breath was knocked out of him, and his ribs felt crushed and broken.

Then the wave rushed back again from the land. It tore Odysseus from his rock, and washed him out to sea. Pieces of skin, torn from his fingers, clung to the blood-stained rock like limpets.[1]

Odysseus saw that if he stayed where he was, the next huge wave would smash him to pieces on the rocks. He swam out into deeper water, and then made his way along the coast, looking for a safer place to land.

At last he came to a river-mouth. The river ran out to sea across gentle, sandy beaches.

Odysseus struggled inshore, against the current. He hauled himself up on the sand, out

[1] limpet: a small shellfish that clings to rocks.

of reach of the snarling sea. With his last strength he undid the veil, and let the river-current carry it back to Athene.

Then he collapsed, totally exhausted. He was naked, starving and alone in a strange land. But he'd got there by his own strength and cunning. Poseidon had held him back, but hadn't been able to stop him.

He rested his torn, battered body on the sand. The skin on his hands had been torn away, and they burned in red-hot agony from the salt water. He was as naked and helpless as a newborn baby. And like a newborn baby, he laid his head down, and slept.

Nausikaa

King Alkinoös of Phaiakia had a beautiful daughter. Her name was Nausikaa. While Odysseus lay on the beach, sleeping his exhaustion away, Nausikaa, in her palace bedroom, was having a troubled dream.

In the morning she went to her father, in the great hall of the palace.

'Father,' she said, 'last night I was troubled by a dream. A messenger from the gods came to me, and disturbed my sleep.'

'What was the message?'

'Simply this. You're a great king, with many people to rule. And I have several grown-up brothers – young princes without a care in the world. In the palace store-rooms we've robes and tunics of the finest cloth. But they are lying there going mouldy, because no one wears them and looks after them.'

'What d'you want to do?'

'Please give orders for a strong mule-cart to be got ready. I'll load all the clothes on to it. Then I'll take them down to the seashore, and wash them. That way they'll look like new, and you and your sons can dress as a king and princes should.'

King Alkinoös smiled. He was a wise man, and guessed the part of Nausikaa's dream she hadn't mentioned. The gods had whispered in her ear that it was time to think of her own wedding. The royal robes would be part of her dowry.

'Of course, my dear,' he said. 'Get your slaves to collect the clothes, and I'll have a mule-cart brought up right away.'

Nausikaa hurried away to organise her slaves. Alkinoös ordered a mule-cart to be brought into the palace courtyard.

Nausikaa and her slaves loaded the cart with the clothes from the store-room. They took a box of food, and a skin of wine, so that they could spend all day at the beach. Nausikaa took a silver flask of scented olive-oil, so that she and her maids could bathe, and anoint themselves when the washing was done.

It was a fine, sunny morning. The cart was loaded, and the mules set off. Nausikaa rode in the driver's seat, while her maids walked beside her.

They followed the river, down to the sea. Not far from the estuary, it spread out into deep, dark pools of fresh water. The maids took the clothes and put them into these pools, treading them down and rinsing them carefully, till no dirt was left.

When the clothes were washed, they spread them on the beach, to dry in the sun. Then they stripped and bathed.

After they'd bathed, they rubbed themselves with soft olive-oil, and dressed. Then they sat down to a picnic of bread, cheese and fruit, which they washed down with Alkinoös' best wine.

When they'd eaten and rested, Nausikaa and her maids took a ball from the mule-cart. While they waited for the clothes to dry, they played 'catch'. As they played, Nausikaa led them in a song.

It was this singing that woke Odysseus, on the other side of the river. He opened his eyes, and stared in amazement at the girls. Wherever had they come from?

One of them threw the ball too hard. Nausikaa missed it, and it fell into the river. Laughing and shouting, the girls ran to the bank to fetch it.

'What shall I do?' thought Odysseus to himself. 'Who are these girls? Mortals, or sea-nymphs like Kalypso? Whoever they are, I must go and speak to them. I need food, and shelter, or I'll die of exposure.'

He was naked, and filthy. Salt and sand caked his body. Strips of skin had been torn from him, leaving angry, red flesh. His hair and beard were tangled and matted, from the battering Poseidon had given him. How could he appear like this before these young girls, without frightening them away?

He hesitated a moment. Then he broke off a leafy branch, to hide his nakedness. Holding it in front of him, he walked forward to the river bank. He was like a starving lion, forced to come out of his lair to hunt, or die.

The slave-girls saw him, and screamed in terror. They ran away. Only Nausikaa stood firm. She and Odysseus faced each other over the swirling river.

'Lady,' said Odysseus, 'whether you're a mortal or a sea-nymph, take pity on me. I'm naked, alone and helpless. I've been eighteen days lost at sea, and spent the last two swimming for my life. You're the first person I've seen in all that time. Please help me.'

'Sir,' answered Nausikaa, 'of course I'll help you. My name is Nausikaa, and I'm a princess of Phaiakia. My father, King Alkinoös, welcomes all strangers to our country.'

She turned to her maids, who were fearfully keeping their distance.

'Come back, you silly girls! Anyone would think you'd never seen a man before!'

'Lady,' said Odysseus, 'I understand why they're afraid. Leave some clothes on the bank, and some olive-oil to rub myself with, when I've washed. Then, when I'm dressed, I shan't be so ashamed to talk to you, or so frightening to your maids.'

Nausikaa did as he asked. She laid a cloak and tunic on the river bank, and put the flask of olive-oil beside them. Then she went off with her maids, and left Odysseus alone.

He swam across the river. Then, groaning as the water ran over his cuts and bruises, he washed all the salt and filth from his body. He rinsed his hair and beard, and combed them out. He rubbed himself with olive-oil, and dressed in the fine clothes Nausikaa had left him.

When he'd finished, he stood there, handsome as a god. The fierce, naked wanderer had gone, and in his place stood a king of men.

Meanwhile Nausikaa and her maids had gathered the dry clothes together, and piled them into the cart. Nausikaa saw that

Odysseus was dressed, and came across to him.

'Sir, you must be starving after all you've suffered. We have food and wine to spare. When you've eaten, come back to my father's palace. For I can see that you're a noble lord, not a pirate or a robber.'

'Thank you,' said Odysseus.

He sat down on the beach, and the slave-girls brought him meat, bread and wine. He ate and drank ravenously, for he'd had nothing for two days – not since the beginning of the storm.

When he'd finished, and everything was loaded in the cart, Nausikaa spoke again.

'Sir,' she said, 'while we're out of sight of the palace, you can walk with the girls, beside the cart. But once we come in sight of it, you must leave us, and go into the palace by yourself.'

'Why?' asked Odysseus in surprise.

'What would people think, if they saw me coming back with a stranger in tow? "Nausikaa wants to get married. Our young men aren't good enough for her. So she goes off to the beach, and picks up the first wanderer she finds there!" That's what they'd say.'

'What should I do instead?'

'Leave us time to get into the palace, and

then walk in on your own. Pretend you've just landed here, and have come to visit the king. Throw yourself on my father's mercy. We're always glad to help strangers.'

Odysseus agreed to this plan. The sun was setting as Nausikaa flicked the mules with her whip, and they set off up the royal road to the palace.

When they came in sight of it, Odysseus left Nausikaa and her maids to go on alone. He went into a grove of trees, sacred to Athene, and prayed to her.

'Athene, unsleeping daughter of Zeus, hear my prayer. Let King Alkinoös and his people welcome me kindly, and not turn me away. Let yesterday's storm be the last torment I have to suffer.'

Athene heard his prayer. But her uncle Poseidon was still angry, and she was afraid to appear before Odysseus, or answer him.

Odysseus waited a while, but there was no sign. With a heavy heart, he left the grove and walked up to the palace of King Alkinoös.

Alkinoös

While Odysseus was praying to Athene, Nausikaa and her maids had reached the palace. Nausikaa's brothers came out to meet her. They unharnessed the mules, and led them to their stables. Nausikaa went inside, up to the women's quarters. Her old nurse was there. She helped the Princess bathe, and lit a warm fire in her room. The slaves brought food and wine, and set it on a polished table, for Nausikaa's supper.

Meanwhile Odysseus, too, had come into town. He met a young girl, with a water-jug on her shoulder.

'Excuse me, my dear,' he said, 'but can you tell me the way to King Alkinoös' palace?'

'Follow me,' said the girl.

Odysseus looked into her eyes. They were deep-set, and dark as the pools in a mountain stream.

Athene had heard his prayer after all. With relief in his heart, he followed her.

Athene led him through the town to the

king's palace. A mist of invisibility shrouded them. None of the townspeople saw them as they went.

At the palace gate, Athene stopped.

'Now, sir,' she said, 'the rest is up to you. This is King Alkinoös' palace. The king and his noblemen are holding a great feast tonight. Go in fearlessly, and bow down in front of Alkinoös. Answer all his questions. He'll help you in your journey.'

With that, she left him. She soared up into the evening sky, like a bird, and disappeared.

Odysseus offered her thanks. He walked into the palace. As he went, he felt the mist of invisibility vanish. The guards stared at him in amazement. Who was this handsome stranger? Where had he appeared from so suddenly?

Odysseus went straight into the great hall of the palace, across to the throne, where Alkinoös sat. As he went, silence fell. Everyone stopped eating and drinking, and watched him. No one tried to stop him.

Odysseus knelt before King Alkinoös. 'My lord,' he said, 'I'm at your mercy, and I ask for your help. I'm a wanderer, and the gods have brought me to your kingdom. Please give me shelter, and help me on my way.'

'Sir,' said Alkinoös, 'we welcome you to

our kingdom. No stranger is ever turned away. When your hunger and thirst are satisfied, you can tell us who you are, and what your business is.'

He signed to the slaves. They brought a throne for Odysseus, and put it beside the king's. The slaves placed a polished table in front of him and put meat and bread and fruit on it. Wine was poured for him in a golden cup.

Odysseus was starving. Eagerly he ate and drank. The feast continued. But as they ate, everyone kept looking at Odysseus. They wondered who he was, and how he'd come to Phaiakia without a ship.

When they'd eaten all they wanted, Alkinoös clapped his hands. The servants cleared the tables. Fresh wine was brought, and the cups filled.

At a signal from the King, two slaves went out to fetch the blind singer Demodokos. The gods had robbed him of his eyes, but given him instead the most beautiful voice a mortal ever owned.

The slaves led Demodokos in, and gave him his lyre[1] of polished tortoise-shell. He began to play, and everyone listened with

[1] lyre: a musical instrument with strings like a harp, but small enough to hold in the hand.

pleasure. No one in all the world could play and sing like Demodokos.

He sang of the Trojan War. He told how Paris had stolen Helen, the wife of King Menelaos. The Greeks went to Troy, to fetch her back. For years they besieged the city. It was only after ten years, when many brave heroes had died on each side, that they were successful. Odysseus had suggested a cunning plan which was to make a wooden horse, fill it with Greek soldiers, and leave it on the plain, for the Trojans to drag into their city.

As Odysseus listened, he remembered the war, and all the brave deeds done there. He remembered the proud Trojans, and his friends who had died fighting them. Tears sprang into his eyes. He was ashamed, in case Alkinoös saw them. He covered his eyes with his hand, until Demodokos finished the song.

No one noticed except Alkinoös. Everyone else was enjoying the singing. But the king saw how the song had affected the stranger. When Demodokos stopped, and the cheering died away, Alkinoös got up, and went to Odysseus.

'Sir,' he said, 'why are you weeping? Is the memory of the war so dreadful, that you can't bear to hear about it, even in a song? What's the matter? Who are you?'

'My lord Alkinoös,' answered Odysseus, 'that song is my song. The heroes who died were my friends. I fought in that war. Now I'm alone, a weary traveller far from home. I beg you to help me. Give me a ship and a crew, and let them take me home.'

'Of course,' said Alkinoös. 'No traveller ever asks for help in vain. But you must tell us who you are. How did you get away from Troy? Why has it taken you ten years to get here?'

'It's a long story. Too long to tell in one night.'

'Never mind. It will take some days to get a ship ready, and find a crew. Begin your story now. You can finish it tomorrow. Tell us all your adventures, from the fall of Troy until you reached Phaiakia today. Begin at the beginning, and leave nothing out.'

Nobody

Everyone in the great hall watched Odysseus as he began his story.

'My lord Alkinoös,' he said, 'I'll tell you everything. My name is Odysseus, son of Laertes. My home is in Ithaka. I fought in the Trojan War. It was my idea to build the wooden horse, and trick the Trojans. The gods helped us beat them, and destroy their city.

'When Troy fell, we divided up the prisoners and treasure, and set sail for home. I had ten ships, six hundred men. We didn't know, when we set out, that none of us would ever reach our homes. The gods were against us. I've been a wanderer for the last ten years. I'm alone. I've lost my ships, my treasure, my men – everything. No mortal can fight the gods, and hope to win.

'We set sail from Troy, leaving the city a blackened ruin. The wind carried us to Ismaros, where the Kikonians live. They had helped the Trojans and were our enemies. We attacked their city, and took many prisoners.

'But some of them escaped. They fled to the hills. In the villages there, they collected an army. They came back at night, and attacked us as we slept.

'The battle was fierce, and long. In the end they forced us right back to the seashore. We put to sea, and quickly sailed away, leaving our enemies cheering on the beach. Six men from each of my ships were dead.

'That night a storm blew up. It raged for nine days and nights. Poseidon, god of the sea, was angry with us. He battered our ships with waves like mountains. The sky was black, and the winds drove us wherever they pleased.

'On the tenth day the storm went, as fast as it had come. We looked up into clear blue sky. No one knew where we were. A low coastline lay ahead. There were green fields, and farmhouses with smoking chimneys. Eagerly we rowed our battered ships to land.

'That place was the country of the Lotoseaters. They're a lazy, peaceful people. They sit about all day, chewing lotos-fruits. Lotosfruits are a drug. They make men slow and lazy. Once you taste the fruit you forget your wife, your home, your friends. All you want to do is stay forever in peaceful Lotos-land, eating the fruit of the lotos-tree.

'Several of my men tried the drug, for a laugh. But once they'd tried it, they were hooked, like fish on a line. When I went to tell them it was time to leave, they stared at me with empty eyes. They didn't recognise me at all.

'We dragged them back to the ships. They were slowed down by the drugs and didn't fight back. But they wept, and begged us to leave them with their new friends, the Lotos-eaters.

'We refused to listen, and set sail at once. After a few days, we came to another island. Its fields were full of nodding corn. The pastures were filled with sheep and cattle. There was a broad river running down towards the sea. On each side stood tall poplars, and soft willows. It was a lovely place, blessed by the gods.

'We should have known better than to land. When the gods bless a place, it's never safe for strangers. But we were tired and hungry. We beached our ships, and I gathered the crews on the shore.

' "Stay here," I said to them. "Remember the Kikonians and the Lotos-eaters. It could be dangerous here, too. I'll take a party of twelve men and explore. The rest of you wait here. Be ready to set sail at once, if there's any trouble."

'Grumbling, they agreed. I picked twelve of my best men. While they got ready, I went to the ship, and took out a goatskin bottle of fine red wine. It was a present to me from a priest of Apollo – the finest wine in the world, fit even for gods. It was so rich, that you had to mix one cup of it with twenty cups of water before you drank. I thought it would make a good present for the king of the island.

'The party of explorers set off, leaving the rest of the men on the beach, beside the ships. We went upriver into the hills. We saw no one.

'At last we came to a huge cave, in the side of a cliff. There was no one about. We went inside, and found that it was someone's home. There were pens full of sheep and lambs, and the floor was covered with bowls of creamy milk, and cheese in wicker baskets. There was a huge table, twice as high as a man, with massive chairs set round it.

'My men wanted to steal some cheese and milk, and take enough sheep back to the ships for everyone. But I said no. We'd wait and meet the owner.

'I should have done as they suggested. But the gods made me stupid. We lit a fire, killed one of the sheep, and made a meal of mutton, cheese and milk. Then we sat and waited for the cave's owner to come home.

'At last he came. We shrank back in horror, and hid in the shadows when we saw him. He was a giant. He had only one eye, and that was in the middle of his forehead. He was Polyphemos, the most savage of all the Cyclopes.

'Polyphemos was carrying a huge bundle of firewood. He tossed it down with a crash. Then he drove his sheep into the milking-pens. Carefully, he milked each ewe, and put her own lamb to suck. He left some of the milk in pails, to drink with his supper. He curdled the rest, and put it in wicker baskets to make cheese.

'When all the ewes were milked, Polyphemos took a gigantic stone, the size of a small ship, and placed it over the cave-mouth. It would have taken fifty men to lift it. We were trapped.

'Next, Polyphemos stirred up the fire. In its light he saw us, cowering in the corner of the cave.

' "Strangers!" he said. "Who are you? Where are you from?"

' "We're Greeks," I answered, "travelling home from Troy."

' "Where are your ships? How many men have you?" he asked.

'A cold shiver ran down my back. I knew it was a trick. The gods helped me, and sent me a lie to protect my men. "They're all lost," I said. "Our ships have been wrecked, and everyone drowned. We're the only survivors. We ask you to help us, in the name of Zeus."

' "The name of Zeus?" he echoed. "We Cyclopes aren't afraid of Zeus. We're just as strong as he is. Look!"

'Without another word, he grabbed two of my men, and bashed their brains out on the stone floor. Then he tore them apart, limb from limb, and ate them. We watched, still as statues, sweating with terror.

'He crunched the last bone, and licked the warm blood from his lips. He took a huge drink of milk.

' "That's better," he said. "Now I'm full, and I feel sleepy. Leave me in peace – or else!"

'He lay down, and was soon snoring. At once my men began weeping and crying, asking me what to do. I didn't know. I thought of drawing my sword, and stabbing him where he lay. But then I remembered the huge rock over the cave-mouth. That was no use. We'd never be able to move it ourselves. Our only hope was to trick Polyphemos into moving it. But how? We were trapped, and helpless.

'None of us slept that night. Next morning, at dawn, Polyphemos got up. He stretched and yawned. Then he snatched two more of my men, and ate them for breakfast. He unlocked the cave-mouth, led his sheep outside, and put the stone back, leaving us inside.

'Once again my men crowded round, asking what to do. Their eyes were white with terror.

'I went over to Polyphemos' bundle of firewood. I found a thick branch two metres long. It was straight, and about fifteen centimetres thick. I sharpened the end to a point with my sword. Then I heated it in the fire, till it was black, and hard as stone.

'I explained the plan to my men. It was dangerous, but there was nothing else we could do. We sat waiting for evening. Our teeth rattled with fear. No one said anything.

'When evening came, Polyphemos came back. He unblocked the cave, drove his sheep inside, and replaced the stone. He milked the sheep as before, and put the lambs beside their mothers.

'Then he grabbed two of my men, and killed them for supper. This was my chance. I stepped forward. In my hand I held the goat-skin bottle of wine.

' "Cyclops," I said. "I've a present for you. Some wine to go with your meal. Here it is."

'Polyphemos took the bottle, uncorked it, and sniffed.

' "Very nice," he said. "Tell me your name, and I'll give *you* a present."

'I thought quickly.

' "Cyclops," I said, "my name's Nobody. What present will you give me?"

'He answered with a cruel joke.

' "Nobody, eh? Well, this is your present. Of all the men here, I'll eat Nobody last of all."

'He started his revolting supper. As he drank the strong wine, he grew drunker and sleepier. At last he lay down, and fell into a drunken sleep. He belched, and lumps of human flesh, mixed with milk and wine, spewed out on to the floor of the cave.

'When I was sure he was sound asleep, I gave the sign to my men. We took the sharpened pole, and heated it in the fire till it was red-hot. Then we went over to the Cyclops. Quickly my men stabbed it into his one eye. I leaned on it from above, twisting it round like a drill.

'His eye sizzled and boiled, and he screamed in agony. We jumped back and hid. Blindly he rushed round the cave, trying to find us. But he was too full of agony, and too drunk, to get us. He screamed and screamed, banging his head against the wall in agony.

'The other Cyclopes came running up, outside the cave.

' "What's the matter, Polyphemos?" they called. "Why are you screaming?"

' "It's Nobody's fault," groaned Polyphemos. "Nobody's here in the cave with me. Nobody's hurt my eye."

' "Well, if nobody's there, what's all the fuss about? Shut up and let us sleep."

'They went away. Polyphemos sat down by the rock across the cave-mouth, grinding his teeth with pain. He felt the ground all round him, trying to catch us.

'Now, I put the second part of my plan into action. I took each of my men across to the sheep-pen. I took three of the biggest sheep, and tied them together. Under the belly of the middle sheep, I tied a man. When they were all hidden, I went to the leader of the flock, a beautiful ram with a fine, long fleece. I lay down beside him, to wait for morning.

'As soon as it was dawn, Polyphemos unblocked the cave-mouth, to let his sheep go to the pasture. But he stayed there, feeling each animal as it passed. He meant to stop us escaping.

'I watched, holding my breath, until the last of my men were outside. Then I grabbed hold of the fleecy ram underneath, and hung on under its belly. It walked slowly to the cave-mouth.

'Polyphemos felt it with his huge hand. ' "Ram," he said, "why are you last today? You usually lead the flock. Are you sad because your master's eye is lost? Nobody did this, and Nobody's going to pay. Go out and lead the flock to the pasture. Leave me to search the cave."

'He let the ram go, and I breathed again. The ram trotted out of the cave. Polyphemos blocked the entrance with the huge rock. I could hear him cursing and groaning inside, as he began to search the cave.

'Quickly I stood up, and freed my men. We ran back to the shore, driving all the fattest sheep ahead of us.

'I was glad I'd told the others to keep the ships ready to sail. We ran down the beach, put the sheep on board, and jumped in ourselves.

' "Cast off, quickly!" I shouted. "Row as fast as you can! We must get out of here!"

'My crews bent to the oars. Soon we were

far enough out to sea to be safe from the Cyclopes. I looked back. On the mountain-ridge stood Polyphemos, with a group of Cyclopes. They were all as tall as trees, and furious that they couldn't catch us. Their angry roars were like rocks rumbling down a hillside.

' "Polyphemos!" I shouted with all my strength. "My name isn't Nobody. It's Odysseus, King of Ithaka. You killed my men, and I punished you!"

'Polyphemos didn't answer. Instead he picked up a stone the size of a house, and flung it at us. It crashed into the sea beside my ship. The tip of it caught the steering-oar, and my helmsman was flung overboard and drowned.

'I ran to the steering-oar.

' "Quickly! Before he can throw another!" I shouted.

'My men beat the water to foam. We didn't relax till we were out of range, and the island of the Cyclopes was nothing but a blur on the horizon.'

Pig men

When Odysseus finished his story of the Cyclopes, everyone sat still. They were all too horrified to say anything.

At last Alkinoös spoke.

'Odysseus,' he said, 'that was a dreadful adventure. No one has ever told us a story like that before. Was that the worst you suffered? Did the gods leave you alone after that?'

'No,' answered Odysseus. 'There was far worse to come. All my men died, because of their own stupidity. I was the only one who escaped.'

'How did they die? You were out at sea, safe from the Cyclopes. What happened?'

'For a time we thought the gods were on our side,' said Odysseus. 'We sailed along with the wind behind us, until we reached the island of Aiolos, the King of the Winds. The gods are afraid of him, and keep him safe and happy. Anyone who rules the winds has power over the whole world.

'Aiolos was pleased to see us. He let us

stay for a month, feasting and resting after our terrible adventures.

'At last the day came for us to leave. My men began loading the ships. Aiolos took me on one side.

' "Odysseus," he said, "I've a present for you. In this bag are some of my winds. It's tied with a special knot, so that they can't get out. Open it when you need help. I've told them to speed you on your way, and then to hurry home to me. The winds will do as you tell them. But only you."

'I thanked Aiolos, and loaded the bag with the rest of the cargo. We said goodbye, and set sail.

'After nine days we were so near home that we could see the fires and houses of Ithaka. I was exhausted. I'd been steering for nine days and nights. Thinking we were safe at last, I relaxed. The gods sent sleep to my eyes.

'While I slept, my stupid crew began grumbling.

' "What's so special about Odysseus?" they said to each other. "We've suffered just as much as he has. Why should Aiolos give him a special present? And what's in the bag anyway? Let's open it while he's asleep, and see."

'The fools! They couldn't untie the knot,

so they cut the cord. At once all the winds rushed out, like roaring lions or stampeding cattle. They had no master and they whirled about us in the night sky. Our ships spun round helplessly, and rushed through the waves. No one knew where we would end up.

'At last, after six days, the winds grew tired of their game. They went back to King Aiolos. But we were totally lost, drifting helpless on the flat, calm sea.

'At last, in the distance, I saw land on the horizon. I ordered my fools of a crew to row. By evening we'd reached it. We beached the ships and disembarked. We made driftwood fires on the beach and ate and drank. Everyone was scared. We didn't know where we were. Everyone was thinking of the Cyclops. Were we back on his island? Or somewhere even worse? We slept under the stars – those of us who could get to sleep at all.

'Next morning, I divided the men into two groups. One group was led by Eurylochos. They went inland, to see who lived on the island. The other group stayed by the ships, with me.

'We waited all day, worried about the men who'd gone with Eurylochos. I began to wonder if we'd ever see them again.

'Then, as it was getting dark, a single

figure appeared in the shadows. In the flickering firelight we saw his pale face, and his eyes white with fear. It was Eurylochos. He was alone.

'His face was scratched and dirty, where trees had caught him as he ran. Tears were pouring down his cheeks. He was panting for breath, and could hardly speak.

' "Dead!" he gasped. "They're all dead! Get away from here, quickly!"

' "What happened?" I said. "Calm down and tell us, whatever it is."

'Gradually he quietened, and we got his story out of him.

' "We came to a palace," he said. "It was in the middle of rich fields and fertile orchards. The mistress of the house was called Kirke. She asked us in, and gave us a feast of rich food and fine wine.

' "But when we'd finished eating, she . . . she touched each man with a magic wand, and at once they changed into pigs. They grew snouts and hooves, bristles and tails. But inside they were still men. Human tears ran down their pigfaces, as Kirke drove them into a sty with all the other human animals."

' "How did you get away?"

' "As soon as I saw what was happening, I

74

hid. Then I ran, as fast as I could. I didn't look back, until I was safely here. Sail away, Odysseus! Sail away, before we're all turned into pigs!"

' "No!" I said angrily. "I won't sail away, and leave half my crew in Kirke's pig-sties. Tomorrow, if the gods help, I'll rescue them myself!"

'I forced my men to lie down and rest. But I couldn't sleep myself. I sat by the fire on the beach, hugging my knees and thinking.

'Suddenly, in the shadow of the trees, I saw something move. I snatched up my spear, and sat tense and ready. Like smoke, a small cloud billowed out of the shadows, and grew bigger. Soon it was the size of a man.

'The hair on my neck prickled. The smoke was growing arms, legs and a head. My spear clattered on the ground. The shadow-figure grew clearer. It slid towards me, swirling in the breeze. A cold chill filled the beach.

'The figure was one of the gods themselves.

' "Odysseus!" it said, in a chilling whisper. "Don't be afraid. I'm Hermes, Guide of the Dead. I've come to help you. Take this drug. It will keep you safe from Kirke's poison tomorrow. When she sees that she can't change you into a pig, she'll be afraid, and do whatever you ask.''

'The god gave me a thin, twisted root. His smoky hand was as cold as ice. I took the root, and he vanished, into the dark sky with the firesmoke.

'I felt exhausted. I didn't even ask myself whether Hermes was friendly or not. I lay down beside the fire, and fell asleep at once.

'Next morning, I was up at dawn. I checked that the root was still tucked into my belt. I picked up my spear, and slung a sharp sword from my shoulders.

'My crew gathered round me.

' "Odysseus," they said, "let us come with you. Don't leave us here alone."

' "No," I answered. "I must go alone. Stay here – and be ready to sail."

'They grumbled, but did as I told them. I hurried through the wood till I came to the palace. There were pens and cages all round it, filled with enchanted animals. They stretched out their paws as I went by. Tears ran down their faces.

'Inside, I heard a woman singing. I followed the sound, and came to an inner room. There was a loom set up, and Kirke was weaving on it, singing as she worked. Grey smoke gusted up around her, as if she was working on a cloud. The room was cold as the sea.

'As soon as she saw me, she jumped up.

' "Welcome, stranger!" she said. "Sit down and eat and drink. After that, I've got something to give you."

'She clapped her hands, and food and drink appeared on a table. There were no slaves, no beings of any kind at all. She had produced the food by magic.

'Carefully, while Kirke wasn't looking, I slipped Hermes' drug into the wine.

'When I'd finished eating and drinking the cold food, Kirke came up behind me. Her breath was cold as death on my neck. She tapped me sharply with a magic wand.

' "Get up!" she said. "Into the sty, with the other pigs."

'I stood still, waiting to see if Hermes had helped me or cheated me. Nothing happened. I stayed as I was – a man. The drug had worked.

'When Kirke saw that I hadn't turned into a pig, she fell on her knees in fright.

' "Sir," she said, "don't hurt me! You must be one of the gods themselves. What can I do to help you?"

' "I'm no god," I answered. "I'm Odysseus,

King of Ithaka. Set my men free, along with all your other prisoners, and let us go. If you don't, I'll kill you."

' "Odysseus!" she said. "The gods told me you'd come. They told me to do whatever you wanted."

' "Then set my men free."

' "First, I must give you a message, from Zeus himself. Before you continue your journey, you must go down to the Underworld. This island is warm and welcoming, compared to the chill there. Ghosts live there. Look for the ghost of the prophet Teiresias. He'll tell you the future. You must do this, if you want to get home alive."

' "How will I get there?"

' "Zeus has ordered me to show you the way. But first, I'll set your men free."

'She led me out to the pens and cages. She touched each animal with her wand, and muttered some magic. Her voice was like a whisper in a graveyard. At once, like ice melting in a fire, the animal-disguise left the men. They stood upright, blinking in the warm sunlight, and stretching their cramped arms and legs.

' "Quickly, Odysseus!" said Kirke. 'Hurry back to the ships. The magic soon forms again, like ice. Sail to the River of Ocean, and the Rivers of Fire and Weeping. That's where Teiresias is waiting."

'I wasted no time.

' "Come on!" I shouted to my crew, hurrying off through the wood, leaving them to follow. They rushed after me – and so did all the other beast-men that Kirke had set free.

'We were in such a hurry that we didn't notice Elpenor. He was a silly lad, about fifteen and not too bright. He ran so fast to follow us that he didn't notice a deep hole full of ice and stones. He fell in, and broke his neck. And we were in such a hurry, we didn't notice. We ran back to the ships, and jumped in.

' "Cast off!" I shouted. "Row as hard as you can! The magic mustn't catch up up!"

'The crews bent to the oars, and we set course for the three rivers, as Kirke had told us. I shivered at the thought of them. The River of Ocean, the River of Fire, and the River of Weeping. Each one sounded worse than the last.'

Ghosts

'As soon as Kirke's island was out of sight, a strong wind blew up. We were driven ahead of it. There was no need to row, no need to steer. The gods were blowing us where they wanted.

'We came at last to the River of Ocean, on the edge of the world. There, the sea and land are covered in wet, drifting mist, and a huge waterfall boils as the sea falls off the edge of the world. Spray hangs above it, like a sodden curtain. There is no sunlight. Everything is dark and gloomy. Night rules – night and grey fear.

'We landed on the slimy beach. I dug a trench in the wet earth, a metre wide and five metres long. As I dug, foul-smelling water oozed up through the muddy floor. We sacrificed sheep and goats to the Dead, and let the blood of the sacrifice run into the trench.

'As soon as the ghosts smelled the fresh blood, they began sliding up from the Underworld. Young girls, babies, old men and women, heroes with their battle wounds still hanging open. They clustered up to the trench, rustling like leaves in the wind. They longed for the blood.

'I drew my sword.

' "Get back!" I shouted. "No blood for any ghost, until I speak with Teiresias!"

'They drew back, their eyes glinting with fear, and their lips curled with hatred. Ghosts are afraid of living steel.

'Then, in the crowd, I saw Elpenor. His head sagged to one side of his broken neck. Tears ran down his grey cheeks.

' "Elpenor!" I called. "What are you doing there? Come up and speak to me."

'He made a helpless sign with his hands. He would have shaken his head, except for his broken neck. He looked sideways at me, and pointed to the blood in the trench. His mouth opened and shut like a fish gasping for life.

'I saw what he wanted. Ghosts can't speak, unless they drink fresh blood first. Until then, only other ghosts can hear them.

' "Come to the trench, then, and drink!" I said.

'Elpenor took a long sip of blood. A single spot of red colour shone in his grey cheeks.

' "My lord Odysseus," he said, in a creaking voice, like a dead tree groaning in the wind. "Please bury me! Until my body's buried, I have to wander here on the shore for ever."

' "But when did you die? And how?"

' "I fell into a hole, at Kirke's place, and . . . broke . . . my . . . n . . ."

'His voice grew faint as the blood ran out. I signed to him to take another sip. As he drank, the veins on his face glowed dull red, like the veins in a dead, autumn leaf.

' "Bury me, Odysseus!" he cried out. "Bury me, and end my torture!"

'As he spoke, he grew fainter. The hairs prickled on my neck. I could see right through him. As he faded, he held his hands out, in a last desperate prayer. Then he was gone.

'The other ghosts surged forward, to the blood. But I kept them back with my sword. At last they parted, leaving a lane through the middle.

'In a slow, sad procession, the ghost of the prophet Teiresias came forward. He was surrounded by ghost attendants. As well as being a ghost, he was blind and old.

'He stooped low, and sipped slowly at a handful of blood. Then he stood up straight, and said, in a sad, elderly whisper:

' "Who wants to speak with me?"

' "I do. Odysseus, son of Laertes, King of Ithaka."

' "Odysseus! What brings you here? Why have you come to the edge of the world? Why have you disturbed the Waking Dead? This is the home of shadows. Leave before you're a shadow yourself!"

' "The gods sent me. You're to tell me if I'll ever get home to Ithaka again."

'There was a silence. Teiresias bent, and slowly sipped blood, as if it was delicious wine. His empty eye-sockets glowed, as if there was a fire inside.

' "You'll get home, Odysseus," he said, in his quiet, creaking voice. "Your men will get home too, if you follow my advice. The sheep and cattle of Helios, the Sun-god – you'll find them, feeding peacefully. Don't touch them! Don't kill them, however hungry you are! If you do, your men will never reach home again. Instead, they'll join us here, grey ghosts drained of life."

' "Thank you. We'll do as you tell us."

' "Wait! I said you'll get back home. But your troubles won't be over then. There's a pack of suitors feasting in your palace, like vultures on a dead corpse. You'll have to fight

them, and kill them all. That's ... what ... I
... proph ..."

'His voice ran down, and he faded away,
before he had time to sip more blood.

'I'd heard all I needed. I turned away. At
once, the ghosts rushed at the blood, like a
swarm of grey locusts. As they drank, their
strength came back. We could hear their
voices. They were high and shrill at first, like
twittering bats. But as they grew stronger and
louder, the whole place filled with groaning
and weeping.

'All at once, with a shock of surprise, I
realised that there, among the other ghosts,
were all my friends who'd been killed at Troy.
Achilles, Patroklos, Aias, even King Agame-
mnon himself. They stood there, the wounds
still ragged in their bloodless bodies. Behind
them stood hundreds of dead Greek soldiers,
and a host of Trojans. None of them spoke. They
just stared at me. Tears ran down their cheeks,
but their eye-sockets were hollow and empty.

'There were women and children too. Some
were old, and untouched. But many were
young and pretty. They'd been given to the
soldiers after Troy was captured. Many had
been raped or killed, or roasted alive as their
houses burned. They stood there now, in a

grey huddle. The noise gradually stopped. They looked at me with their sightless eyes. Hatred rose in the air around them, like a foul fog.

'I felt a trickle of panic. Blindly, I turned, and ran. I shouted to my men to cast off and sail away. I could feel the power of the ghosts, like plague-breath, pulling me back to join them. The flesh on my body felt as if it was being ripped from the bones.

'I hurled myself into my ship. We rowed as fast as we could. Behind us grey mist swirled, and covered the slimy land. The ghosts faded from sight. Their voices, their shrill, cursing voices, grew fainter. Soon they disappeared altogether. The roar of the waterfall died away behind us.

'We rowed until at last the sun broke through the clouds. Then we knew we were safe. We hoisted sail, and set our course back to Kirke's island.

'No one spoke. We were all thinking of the sad, grey ghosts. One day each of us would join them. We'd see our long-dead friends again; but our enemies would be waiting too. The thought was like a clammy hand, gripping our hearts, squeezing the life-blood from us.

'We sailed on in silence, till we came to Kirke's island again.'

Monsters

When Odysseus finished telling of the ghosts, King Alkinoös interrupted again.

'Odysseus,' he said, 'whatever did you sail back to Kirke's island for? Surely you'd have done better to keep clear of it?'

'Of course we would,' answered Odysseus. 'But we had Elpenor to think of. We landed at dead of night, and hurried to Kirke's palace. Everything was dark and silent. Now that Kirke's cages were empty, there were no man-beasts to howl as we came nearer.

'We found Elpenor, still lying in the hole where he died. His boy's fuzzy beard had grown on his dead face, like a line of grey mould. We thought we'd taken two days to visit the ghosts. But we'd been away two months. The flesh was sagging off Elpenor's bones. He stank.

'Quickly we dragged out what was left of his body, and buried it in soft sand. Now his ghost would rest at last. We climbed into our ships again, and sailed away. No one had seen us come, and no one saw us leave. The gods were helping us.

'But their help didn't last long. For a while we were driven along by a following wind. But it soon dropped, and we drifted, in a flat calm. No land was visible on any side. The sea was a flat sheet of polished bronze.

'We drifted lazily. Everything seemed safe. But I was uneasy. Calm is dangerous. When things seem safe, the gods are planning trouble.

'A seagull perched on the ship's side, next to me. Its eyes were deep set, dark as pools in a mountain stream. It was Athene.

' "Odysseus, you're in great danger – all of you. You're in the part of the sea ruled by the Sirens. Their singing is so beautiful, that it leads men on to follow them, and their ships are wrecked on jagged rocks. Not far from here is the narrow sea-passage guarded by Skylla and Charybdis. You must face these monsters, and escape from them. Some of your men will be lost. You must make plans now to save the rest."

'Athene flew away. I was full of terror. What could I do – one man against supernatural monsters? I thought for a long time.

'At last, the gods sent me an idea. I stood

up, and shouted so that all the crews could hear:

' "Men, you must do exactly as I tell you, however silly it sounds. Every man is to block his ears with beeswax, so that he can't hear anything. Then you're to tie me tightly to the mast of my ship. Don't unfasten me, or take out the wax, until I give the signal. Start now. Hurry!'

'My men looked surprised, but they trusted me, and did as I told them. They plugged their ears with wax. Then they fastened me tightly to the mast. That way I'd hear the Sirens, but I wouldn't be trapped by them.

'The men rowed slowly on. The sky darkened overhead, and the Sirens appeared. They were huge sea-birds, with women's faces, and human voices.

' "Odysseus!" they sang. "Odysseus, flower of men, heart of the Greeks, come with us. We'll tell you sweet secrets, that no man has ever heard before. Come with us . . ."

'Their singing was the most beautiful sound I'd ever heard. I longed to go with them. I forgot wife, home, son and companions. I felt that unless I went with the Sirens, I'd die. I begged my men, with tears running down my cheeks, to untie me and let me go.

'But their ears were plugged with wax. They couldn't hear the Sirens, and they couldn't hear me either.

'At last the Sirens gave up and flew away. The sky cleared, and the sun came out. I felt drained and empty, like a sucked fruit.

'I signed to my men, and they unplugged their ears. Two of them came and set me free.

' "What happened, Odysseus?" they said, seeing my cheeks wet with tears and my arms and legs raw, where I'd strained at the rope, trying to get free.

' "Nothing I can tell you. It's better for you not to know," I answered. "Now, row on till we reach land."

'Ahead of us was a rocky coastline. There was a narrow channel, in between high cliffs. The water bubbled and frothed, as it was sucked through.

' "We must take that path," I said. "You trusted me before. Do as I tell you, now. Do it at once, if you want to escape this danger, too."

'I'd heard about Skylla and Charybdis, from sailors who'd passed that way before. Skylla is a monstrous dog, ten times the size of a man. She has twelve feet and six snaky necks – each one ending in a head with three rows of teeth, like a shark's. She lives in a cave, high in the cliff-face. As ships pass by, she reaches out, and snatches men to eat alive.

'But Charybdis is even worse. She lives on the sea-bed. She has no body, only an enormous mouth. When ships pass over her lair, she opens her mouth and drinks the sea. Water, ships and crew are swallowed up, and never seen again.

'Soon we were close enough to the channel to see, on the right, the boiling whirlpool over Charybdis' lair. Skylla's cliff was on the left. It looked deserted.

'The current snatched our ships, and began dragging them towards Charybdis.

' "Steer to the right! Row hard!" I shouted.

'My men tugged at the oars, till the veins on their foreheads stood out like knotted cords. Ahead of us, the sea on the right churned round in a boiling hole. Charybdis had opened her jaws.

'Terrified, the men rowed even harder. With great difficulty, we brought the ships past the edge of the hole. We passed Charybdis, but only just. On our right we could see the sand and rocks on the naked sea-bed.

'We stared into the hole, like men in a

trance. Our hands rowed automatically. Our brains froze. Fear was in control.

'Suddenly, there was a dreadful screaming from behind us. We whirled round. Skylla had woken up.

'She reared out from her cave-mouth. Her necks arched out, and each head with its terrible teeth fastened on a man.

'They were lifted up, holding out their hands and screaming with terror. I drew my sword, and ran forward. But there was nothing we could do. The men vanished into Skylla's cave. The screaming stopped, and we heard a dreadful crunching and slobbering as she ate them alive.

' "Row, you fools!" I shouted to the crews. "She'll soon be back! Get us out of here!"

'Desperately they rowed. We passed through the channel, out of range. At last we reached the other side.

'The current caught us, and hurled us on. It smashed the ships hard against a stony beach.

'We were safe. The damage could be repaired. Gratefully we landed, and looked around.

'The beach sloped gently upwards, until it stopped at a line of sand-dunes. Beyond them

91

were rolling fields, fertile orchards, and all the signs of civilisation.

'In the meadows were herds of cattle. They were feeding peacefully. They were broad-browed, strong, with long horns and sturdy legs.

'My heart sank. This was our final test. It was worse than the Sirens, worse than Skylla, worse even than Charybdis.

'These were the cattle of the Sun. To harm them, even to touch them, meant certain and immediate death.'

The cattle of the Sun

Odysseus stopped. He passed a hand wearily over his face.

'My lord,' said Alkinoös quietly, 'we can guess the rest. Your men killed the cattle, and died for it.'

'Not at first,' answered long-suffering Odysseus. 'We had plenty of food and wine on board. For all that day, and the next, we rested. We lit fires and feasted on the shore. Everyone was glad that we'd reached safety at last, and come through all our adventures unharmed.

'But on the third day, Zeus sent a storm. It was black, and violent. It raged for a whole month. The waves were as high as watch-towers. No ship could survive in such a stormy sea. We stayed where we were, huddling together for shelter.

'Soon our food and drink ran out. I kept my men from the cattle of the Sun by force.

'But at last I was so exhausted that I simply

had to sleep. I was so tired that I didn't even dream.

'Eurylochos seized his chance. He'd been against me ever since he'd lost all his men at Kirke's palace. While I slept, he called the men together for a council.

' "Odysseus is destroying us all. This storm will never end, unless we sacrifice to Zeus. Why has he sent a thunderstorm, anyway? Obvious. He wants us to sacrifice, and get back into his favour that way. Look, the Sun won't miss just one bull. We'll wait till he goes behind a cloud, then take the biggest, and sacrifice it to Zeus."

'The men obeyed him. They waited till the Sun was hidden, then killed the biggest bull, and offered him to Zeus. But the smell of roasting meat made them so hungry, that they killed five other bulls, and ate them.

'I woke to the smell of steak.

' "You fools!" I shouted. "Those cattle are sacred. The Sun –"

'A huge crash of thunder interrupted me. The air was filled with blazing sunlight. The Sun was white-hot with anger. A great voice roared out from the sky, and we covered our ears in terror.

' "Zeus!" the Sun screamed. "Zeus, lord Zeus! The mortals have eaten my cattle!

94

Punish them, or I'll never shine again!"

'At once, the sky grew pitch-black. A terrifying thunderstorm began. Zeus was hurling thunderbolts about, like a farmer sowing seeds – seeds of death. One by one the ships were hit. They burned. The smell of sulphur filled the air.

'The men huddled together in a tight, shaking group. That was a mistake. A final rumble of thunder, a rending crash, as if the sky was being split in two. I fell to the ground, screaming. Blood oozed from my tortured eardrums.

'When I got up at last, it was broad daylight. The storm had gone. So had my ships, and all my men. The yellow sand had been scorched white. Wherever I looked, it was empty. The island was a barren, sand-covered desert. There was no sound at all. No men, no animals, no birds. Even the sea was soundless.

'Athene came fluttering down, like a paper seagull. She was the only living thing in sight.

' "Get out of here, Odysseus," she said. "Grab a broken spar, and swim for your life. If you don't, you'll be burned to ash, like a dry, dead twig."

'I didn't hesitate. I stripped, and plunged into the sea. It was scalding hot, from the thunderbolts. I found a broken, blackened piece of mast, and hung on to it. I began to paddle. Athene helped me, smoothing the waves in my path.

'After nine days of drifting, I reached Kalypso's island. I stayed there until the gods told me it was time to leave. Then I built a raft, and sailed here to Phaiakia.

'That's my story, King Alkinoös. No mortal has ever suffered as I have. The gods have taken away my men, my ships, my treasure. They sent me here, a helpless stranger, naked as a newborn child. Please help me. Take me home. Make the last part of my journey to Ithaka easier than the rest.'

He stopped. A murmur of sympathy ran round the hall. Everyone was sorry for him, and wished him well.

King Alkinoös stood up.

'Odysseus,' he said, 'you've suffered more than any man who's ever come to us, asking for help. People of Phaiakia, hear my orders. Each man here will bring our guest a present. Store each present in the hall, in a wooden strong-box, till his ship is ready. Our young men will get ready to sail for Ithaka in three days' time. Meanwhile we'll hold a feast in Odysseus' honour, and make offerings to the gods for his safe return.'

There was a murmur of agreement. Then, as it was late, everyone went home. Next morning, Alkinoös made a sacrifice in honour of the gods. While a feast was being prepared, the young men of Phaiakia began getting a ship ready. They loaded food and wine on board, and placed Odysseus' strong-box carefully in the hold.

The feast went on for three days. On the fourth morning everyone went down to the harbour. Odysseus shook Alkinoös' hand.

'Thank you, my friend. From this day on, Ithaka and Phaiakia will be allies for ever.'

He stepped on board the ship. The young men took their places at the oars. A rug and a pillow had been placed for Odysseus on the deck. Everyone waved goodbye, and prayed to Zeus that this voyage, at least, would not end in tragedy.

The crew unfastened the ship from the stone anchor, and began to row. At once the gods sent a deep sleep on Odysseus' eyes, and he knew nothing more.

The ship sailed on, hissing through the blue water. It was like a team of stallions pulling a fast war-chariot, or a falcon skimming through the air. As Odysseus slept, the care and suffering of ten years' wandering was lifted from him.

Odysseus reaches Ithaka

The ship reached Ithaka. They anchored in a calm bay, and landed Odysseus' strong-box. He was still in the god-sent sleep, and they could not wake him. So they laid him gently on the sand, and sailed home.

Odysseus woke up. He was alone, in a strange land. An orange mist hung over his eyes. He groaned, and sat up.

'O Zeus,' he cried bitterly, 'where am I now? What's the next torture I'm to suffer?'

In answer, Athene came to him, disguised as a shepherd boy. Her deep dark eyes told him who she was at once.

'Odysseus,' she said, 'look around.'

The mist left Odysseus' eyes, and he realised where he was. He fell to his knees. Tears streamed down his cheeks, wetting the long hair that fell over his face. He kissed his native earth, the earth he had not touched for twenty years.

'Long-suffering Odysseus,' said Athene gently, 'everything's not over yet. There are other things to be done. The suitors . . .'

'How?' asked Odysseus. 'I am one man, and they are many.'

'One man, yes – but you are Odysseus the Cunning, Odysseus the King! Use tricks! The gods will help you. Look!'

She touched him with one finger-tip. At once his skin grew old and wrinkled, brown as the skin of an onion. His hair turned thin and grey. His back bent. His new Phaiakian clothes turned to filthy rags.

'There,' Athene said. 'No one will recognise you now, except those you choose to tell. When the time comes, I'll show them the real Odysseus.'

'What have I to do?'

'Whatever you decide. Go up this hill. Eumaios your swineherd lives here. He has stayed faithful to you. He'll recognise you. He'll help you. You'll meet your grown-up son, Telemachos, at his hut, too.'

'Telemachos! Why can't I show him who I am?'

'When the time is right. Go now. I'll hide your strong-box, where no one will find it.'

She disappeared, like a puff of mist. Odysseus looked around. Twenty years was a long time, but he was beginning to remember where he was. In front of him lay the path to Eumaios' hut.

He cut himself a stick to lean on. Then, slowly, the bent, ragged wanderer started up the path. It was steep and stony. But he didn't notice. All he felt was joy. He was coming home at last.

Eumaios

When Odysseus reached the swineherd's hut, he found Eumaios in the courtyard. He was cutting himself a new pair of sandals from a piece of pig-skin. His servants had gone out, with the pigs, to the woods where they fed. One man had gone to town, with a fat hog for the suitors' supper.

As soon as Odysseus walked into the courtyard, Eumaios' guard dogs rushed at him, barking and snarling. At once Odysseus sat down, and dropped his stick. He kept very still. He knew that if he moved, the dogs would rip his throat out.

Eumaios saw what was happening. He dropped the leather, and ran over. He cuffed and kicked the dogs out of the way. Whining, they slunk back to the shelter of the wall.

'You were lucky that time, old man,' said Eumaios. 'If you hadn't had the sense to sit down, you'd be dead by now.'

Odysseus didn't say anything.

'Well,' went on the swineherd, 'You're

welcome, whoever you are. I welcome every wanderer who comes here, because of my master Odysseus. He's been a wanderer for twenty years. I hope other people are as friendly to him as I am to every stranger who comes to Ithaka.'

He led Odysseus inside, and sat him down in a wicker chair covered with shaggy goatskin. Then he went to the pig-sties, and chose a fine young piglet. He slaughtered it, cut it up, and roasted it for his guest.

When everything was ready, he put the meat on a table beside Odysseus. There was bread and wine as well.

'Eat well, my friend! This is my master's food, but he would welcome you, if he was here. When you've eaten, you can tell me who you are, and what you want in Ithaka.'

Odysseus was delighted to see how good a servant Eumaios was. But he still said nothing. As he ate and drank, the swineherd went on with what he was saying.

'If only Odysseus would come back! There's a pack of suitors in his palace. They're eating him out of house and home. Every day, I have to choose my best hogs, and send them down for those useless mouths to eat. If Odysseus came back, we'd soon be rid of them!'

Odysseus finished eating. Eumaios filled their cups with wine, and sat down beside the fire.

'Now sir, tell me who you are, and why you're here.'

It was time for Odysseus to speak. But he didn't know what to say. Did the gods want him to tell Eumaios who he really was, or not? He decided to wait, and test Eumaios to see how far he could be trusted.

'This master of yours, this Odysseus,' he began, 'what did he look like? I may have seen him. I may have news of him. I've been about the world a lot.'

Eumaios burst out laughing.

'That won't work! Every beggar who comes to Ithaka pretends he's bringing news of Odysseus. Penelope and Lord Telemachos have given up listening to them. Once bitten, twice shy, the proverb says.'

'But my news is different. I'm not just saying I *know* Odysseus. I swear to you that he's on his way home. He'll be in Ithaka very soon – and that means trouble for the suitors!'

'I still don't believe you, friend. But don't let's quarrel. It was a good try. Have another drink, and let's stay friends. Forget Odysseus.

103

The gods will bring him back, whenever they choose.'

Odysseus said nothing. His thoughts were full of the honesty of Eumaios, and the dreadful end in store for the suitors.

Eumaios looked into the fire, and held his wine cup closer. He spoke, quietly and bitterly.

'I only wish I *could* believe you. Odysseus has been away so long now, that hardly anyone in Ithaka remembers him. There's only a handful of faithful servants like me, and we've had to leave the town, and take to the hills. I stay here all the year round, and leave it to my men to go into town. Those suitors annoy me – and I don't want to answer back. A servant should know his place.'

The two men sat for a while in silence. Each had his own thoughts. Evening came. As it grew dark, the swineherd's servants came in from the pastures. They drove the pigs into sties for the night, and barricaded the gate. Then they came into the hut, with fresh pork for their supper.

Each man looked curiously at Odysseus. But Eumaios told them he was a visitor, and they greeted him politely, even though he was dressed in filthy rags.

Clearly Eumaios was trustworthy. Odysseus longed to tell him who he really was. But the gods still sent him no sign, and so he said nothing.

The young men finished their food, and went out, yawning and stretching. They had a hut of their own to sleep in. When they'd gone, Odysseus tried again to speak.

'My lord Eumaios,' he began, 'suppose Odysseus *did* come home? What would you do then? Fight on his side, or join the suitors against him?'

'What a stupid question!' Eumaios said angrily. 'Odysseus would be one man, against an army. Anyone who fought with him would be facing certain death. Even so, I'd fight for my master, till I was too weak to stand!'

He stood up. Tears were streaming down his cheeks.

'But let's stop this stupid talk! Odysseus isn't home, and there's no fighting to be done. Let's go to bed, old man. You upset me with all this talk of my master.'

Odysseus said nothing. He'd chosen to speak twice already, and the gods had shown him, each time, that Eumaios wasn't ready to be told.

The swineherd fetched a wooden bed, and

put it down beside the fire. He covered it with the skins of sheep and goats.

'There. You're an old man, and the fire will keep your bones warm tonight. In the morning, you can go to Ithaka, and tell your story to Queen Penelope.'

'But where will you sleep?'

'Outside, guarding the pigs. That's where I always sleep. It's too important a job to leave to my younger men. This herd of pigs must still be the best in Greece, when Odysseus comes back.'

He slung a sharp sword from his shoulders, and wrapped himself in a thick woollen cloak, to keep off the wind. Then he picked up a huge goat's fleece to lie on. His spear was leaning against the doorpost. He said goodnight to Odysseus, and went out.

Odysseus was pleased to see how careful Eumaios was of his master's property. He wrapped himself up, and lay down by the fire. This was his first night in Ithaka for over twenty years. The gods had sent him to Eumaios. Whatever the struggles that lay ahead, he had at least one ally he could trust.

He pulled the covers round him, rested his head on his arm, and was soon asleep.

Telemachos returns

Once Odysseus was safe in Eumaios' hut, Athene flew off to Sparta. It was time for Telemachos to come home to Ithaka.

She found Telemachos and his friend, the prince of Pylos, on the porch of Menelaos' palace. They'd been in Sparta for many days, entertained by Menelaos and Queen Helen. The prince of Pylos was enjoying himself. He didn't have a lost father to worry about. He was fast asleep, and snoring.

But Telemachos wasn't asleep. All the time Odysseus had spent in Phaiakia, telling the story of his wanderings, his son had been waiting in Sparta for news. He'd heard all Menelaos had to tell him, and now he was anxious to get back home. He was sitting on a chair covered with a cloth of royal purple.

Athene disguised herself as one of the palace servants. Then she went silently and stood beside Telemachos' chair.

Telemachos looked into her deep, dark eyes. He jumped to his feet.

'My friend! So the time has come at last!'

'Yes. It's time you went home. There's a lot to be done.'

'I've been waiting for the gods to send me a sign.'

'The sign has come. If you don't get home soon, those suitors mean to divide your wealth between them, and leave you nothing.'

'But what about my mother? What's to happen to her?'

'The rest of her family say she must choose, now. They want her to marry Eurymachos. He's the richest and noblest of the suitors.'

'And the greediest!'

'Yes. Not the man to have as a stepfather. Hurry back. And don't go round by Samos.'

'Why not?'

'The suitors are waiting for you. They're going to ambush your ship and kill you. Keep clear of the islands, and sail at night.'

'At night? But no one ever sails at night!'

'That's why *you* must. No one will be expecting it. The gods will send you a following wind.'

'What must I do when I land in Ithaka?'

'Go straight to Eumaios, the swineherd. He's waiting with news for you.'

Athene vanished, soaring into the air like a

night-flying owl. Telemachos shook his friend awake.

'Come on! We must go! There's no time to waste.'

'Go? In the middle of the night?'

'No! We must get everything ready, and thank Menelaos in the morning. A good host never forgets a polite guest.'

They hadn't long to wait till dawn. As soon as the sun was up, they went to King Menelaos's throne-room.

'I was expecting you,' said Menelaos, before Telemachos could speak. 'The gods sent me a message last night. You must leave. I would have liked you to stay longer, but we must do as the gods tell us.'

He sent for his slaves, and gave them their orders. The queen's slaves went with her to the royal linen-room. There they opened the storage-chests and Helen picked out a beautiful, embroidered robe. She had made it long ago with her own hands. It shone, like a robe of silver stars.

Menelaos went with his steward to the treasury. There he chose a two-handled silver cup, and a silver mixing-bowl. Carrying their presents, the king and queen went back to the throne-room.

'Telemachos,' said Menelaos, 'we have presents for you, in honour of your royal father Odysseus. This cup and bowl are the finest in Sparta. This robe was woven in Egypt, by the queen herself. Take them, in memory of the time when you were a guest of the king and queen of Sparta.'

Telemachos thanked him. The slaves loaded the presents into a chariot. When everything was ready, Telemachos and the Prince of Pylos climbed into the chariot, and set off towards the palace gates.

Menelaos and Helen followed. The king's slaves brought a cup of fresh wine. Menelaos made an offering to the gods, and lifted the cup to his lips.

'Goodbye, young friends. May Zeus bring you safely home. And may he bring you good news of Odysseus!'

In answer to this prayer, Zeus sent them an omen from heaven. A huge eagle flew over the palace. In its talons it carried a snow-white goose. Underneath, the palace slaves ran helplessly along. They cursed and shouted at the bird, but they couldn't catch it. It flew off towards the east, and disappeared.

'There,' said Menelaos. 'That eagle is Odysseus. The goose is the pack of suitors.

110

Just as the eagle dealt with the goose, so Odysseus will deal with the suitors.'

'May the gods bring your prophecy true!' cried Telemachos.

He thanked Menelaos and Helen for their kindness, and touched the horses with his whip. They galloped off through the town, and out across the open country towards Pylos.

Telemachos stayed two nights in Pylos. He feasted with King Nestor, and told him the news from Sparta. While he waited, his crew got a fast ship ready.

The second night, as soon as the sun had set, Telemachos went down to the shore. He said goodbye to Nestor and his son, and ordered the crew to get on board. He sacrificed to the gods of the sea, and to Athene.

The ropes were cast off, and the crew raised the mast and spread the sail. Then they sat down to the oars. All night, they rowed through the darkness. Athene calmed the waves ahead of them, and sent a following wind to swell the sail.

No one ever sails at night. The Sun, who guides men on journeys, is asleep, and the stars are treacherous guides. Storms and rough seas come up unseen at night, and smash ships. But the gods were watching Telemachos, and brought him safely home.

As dawn broke, they reached the coast of Ithaka. They had escaped the dangers of the sea, and the suitors' ambush. They landed. The crew moored the ship with a stone anchor. They took down the sail, and lowered the mast. Then they went ashore.

'Wait here, men, and have breakfast,' said Telemachos. 'Then go round the coast to the town. Don't tell anyone that I'm back in Ithaka. I'm going round my father's estates, to see that everything's in order. I'll come to town as soon as the time is right.'

The crew did as he told them. After they'd eaten, they took to the oars, and rowed off round the headland. Telemachos waited, alone on the beach.

When the ship was out of sight, he looked up into the blue sky. There, hovering overhead, was an eagle. It was like a black dot in the bright sunlight. As he watched, it dipped towards the earth, and flew off inland.

Telemachos bowed his head. The gods had sent another sign. He fastened on his sandals, and slung a sharp sword from his shoulders. Then picking up his spear, he set off up the path towards Eumaios's hut.

Odysseus meets Telemachos

When Telemachos reached the swineherd's hut, Eumaios and Odysseus were eating their breakfast. The swineherd's men had left at dawn, to take the pigs to their feeding-ground.

Telemachos walked into the yard. The dogs, usually so savage with visitors, wagged their tails and nuzzled him. They knew him, and were pleased to see him.

Odysseus looked up, and saw his son. But it wasn't time yet to speak. He touched Eumaios' arm.

'A visitor.'

When Eumaios saw Telemachos, he jumped up and ran to meet him.

'Telemachos! You're safe after all! The suitors were planning to kill you. The gods must have helped you.'

'Yes, I'm safe. What news? Has anything happened since I left?'

'News later. First, breakfast. Come inside.'

He fussed round Telemachos, showing him into the hut, and taking his spear from him. As

Telemachos came in, Odysseus offered him his seat.

Telemachos signed to him to sit down. 'Keep your seat, friend. We're not so short of chairs that we have to make visitors stand.'

Odysseus sat down again. Eumaios bustled about. He made a pile of springy brushwood, and spread a woolly fleece over it. When it was ready, he signed to Telemachos to sit down. He set tables beside them, with meat and bread and fruit. He poured wine into wooden cups.

'There! A breakfast fit for gods.'

They sat and ate the good food hungrily. When they'd finished, Telemachos filled his cup again, and sat back.

'Well, sir,' he said to the visitor. 'Where are you from, and what's brought you to Ithaka?'

'I'm a wanderer, from Crete,' answered Odysseus. 'I came here by ship, alone. I came to ask for your help. Will you let me stay in Ithaka?'

'Stay?' said Telemachos bitterly. 'How can I promise that? There's a pack of suitors feasting in my father's palace. How can I welcome strangers there? I'm ashamed – but one man can't deal with them all.'

'If only Odysseus came back,' said Odysseus, 'he'd deal with them. Or if you asked the people to help –'

'The people? They're afraid of them. We've no open support. Even if Odysseus did come back, we'd still have no one but ourselves to rely on.'

Eumaios got up, very agitated.

'Don't talk about it! I can't bear to think of the way they've treated you! Your mother's been in despair since you left. She thinks the suitors have killed you.'

'In that case, Eumaios, you'd better hurry down to the palace, and tell her I'm safe.'

'Yes – and Laertes, too. Your grandfather's lost all hope. He's hardly eaten or drunk since you left.'

'Tell him as well, then. But don't tell anyone else – especially the suitors. Hurry there, and hurry back.'

Eumaios fastened on his sandals. He took a stout stick, and hurried away towards the town. Telemachos stood at the gate, watching, till he was out of sight.

While Telemachos was out of the way, Athene appeared again to Odysseus. She stood in the middle of the courtyard, like a tall huntress. She was invisible to Telemachos. Only Odysseus could see her – and the dogs. They saw her deep, dark eyes. They whimpered, and lay down trembling, their ears flat against their heads.

'Odysseus,' Athene said, 'the time has come. Shake off your disguise and show Telemachos who you really are.'

She touched Odysseus on the shoulder. At once, his old, wrinkled body changed into a lean, younger one. The dirt vanished, and a healthy tan took its place. His tattered clothes were replaced with a fine new tunic and cloak. The matted grey hair and beard became black and sleek.

Her work done, Athene vanished. Telemachos turned round. When he saw Odysseus, he fell on his knees in awe.

'My lord! You must be one of the gods themselves. Take pity on us! Help us!'

'You're wrong. I'm not a god. I'm Odysseus. I'm your father.'

'No! It's a trick! My father's dead! You changed your appearance by a trick. You must be a wizard, an evil spirit.'

'No. I'm Odysseus. Back after twenty years away. Athene changed me. Look at me, Telemachos! I'm your own father, home again.'

Telemachos looked. The gods cleared his eyes. He knew it was Odysseus.

They flung their arms round each other

and hugged. Tears ran down their cheeks. There was no embarrassment. Father and son were meeting after twenty years apart.

At last Odysseus broke away. He sat down, facing Telemachos.

'Well, he said, 'what shall we do next?'

'Deal with the suitors, father. But how can the two of us fight an army?'

'The gods will help. They brought me back, and they have a plan.'

'What must we do?'

'At dawn tomorrow, go down to the palace. Show yourself to the suitors. Let them see that their murder-plan failed. Later, Eumaios will bring me down. I'll be disguised as a beggar again. The suitors will make fun of me –'

'Not if I can help it!'

'Yes, Telemachos! You mustn't interfere. While they're having their fun, you gather all the weapons from the hall, and hide them. Just leave two swords, and two sharp spears, for us. And find out which of the servants are loyal. Give them weapons, and tell them to wait for a signal. When it comes, this is what to do . . .'

Odysseus and Telemachos went on making plans.

Meanwhile, down in Ithaka, the suitors' ship was back in harbour. They landed,

117

looking foolish.

'What happened? Where's Telemachos?'

'We never even saw him. Perhaps he's drowned –'

At that moment, a messenger galloped through the town on a sweating horse.

'Make room! Make room! A message for Queen Penelope!'

'What message?'

'Her son's come home! Telemachos is back, safely back from Pylos!'

Muttering angrily, the suitors made their way to Odysseus's palace. As they went, Eumaios passed them, leaving the town. He'd delivered his message, and was going back to Odysseus. He saw the suitors, and heard their anger. They were like a swarm of bees disturbed by a greedy bear.

He hurried back to his hut. Odysseus and Telemachos were waiting. Odysseus was disguised as an old beggar again.

'Well, you two,' said Eumaios, 'you seem to have made friends. It's nearly dark. Time for the evening meal. Have you found enough to talk about?'

Odysseus didn't answer. He looked at his son, without winking. Then he got up, and went to help Eumaios prepare the evening meal.

Omens

Next morning, Telemachos was up before the sun. He put on his tunic and sandals, and chose a sharp spear from the rack.

When he was ready, he woke Eumaios up.

'I'm going into the town. My mother's anxious to see me safely back. When our friend wakes up, bring him down to the palace. He can beg there. Someone's bound to help him.'

He said this, knowing that the gods would help Odysseus. They'd see that everything went according to plan.

Telemachos took some bread and grapes, and ate them as he walked. He hurried along, his mind full of the plans he and Odysseus had made. The suitors would soon be finished for good.

Odysseus stayed with Eumaios all day. As soon as the sun began to set, he gathered his belongings together.

'Eumaios, friend, it's time to go.'

The two of them set off – the loyal swineherd and the ragged old beggar. Odysseus leaned on a staff Eumaios had cut for him, as if he found walking hard. Over one shoulder, he wore a dirty, tattered leather bag. All beggars carried them, to hold the food-scraps people gave them.

They went down the rocky path to the town. When they were close enough to see the houses, they stopped to rest. There was a well nearby, with stone seats. It was a meeting-place for the country people.

By the well, they found Melanthios the goat-herd. He was leading some goats and sheep down, for the suitors' supper. He was a swarthy man, with bushy black eyebrows and a squint. The gods had made him ugly to look at, and given him an ugly character too.

'Look at them!' he jeered. 'Birds of a feather! One tattered old crow, leading another! Leave the path to honest men, like me!'

As he passed Odysseus, he aimed a kick at his legs, trying to knock him off the path. Odysseus was furious. He wondered whether to shout his anger, or kill Melanthios where he stood. But Athene was there, invisible. She laid a hand on his shoulder. Odysseus understood, and suffered in silence.

120

'Hah!' sneered the goat-herd. 'Cowards, as well as beggars!'

He swaggered on his way. His friends, the suitors, were waiting for their supper.

When he'd gone, Odysseus and Eumaios set off as well. They went down the hill to the palace. Soon they reached the royal gate.

Just inside, Odysseus stopped.

'What's that?' he asked, pointing his stick at a dark shape in the wall's shadow.

'That? Oh, that's Argos.'

'Argos?'

'Argos, Odysseus's favourite hunting-dog. Poor creature! Once he was the best and bravest of all the royal dogs. But then Odysseus sailed for Troy. That was twenty years ago. Now Argos is old, and blind. He lies there on the dung-heap, hopeless and helpless.'

Odysseus' eyes filled with tears. He began to see what his twenty years away had meant to the people left behind.

He went up to Argos. The dog remembered his master's scent from twenty years before. He stood up, and wagged his tail feebly. His blind eyes shone. A whimper of joy came from his toothless mouth.

Odysseus patted him on the head, then

sadly turned away. There were urgent things to do. Argos would have to wait. He and Eumaios went on their way.

But Argos had got his reward, the reward he had waited for since his master left for Troy. His faithful service was over. He lay down on the dung-heap again, and closed his weary eyes. They would never open again: the gods took him for their own. His loyalty had been rewarded.

Odysseus and Eumaios went into the great hall of the palace. Lamps and pine-torches blazed everywhere, filling the place with light. The golden wine-cups glinted. The feasting suitors' eyes flashed, and sweat gleamed on their foreheads, as they pounded their cups on the tables, calling for the servants.

Telemachos saw the visitors first. Eumaios picked his way towards him, through the rows of boisterous suitors. Odysseus followed, humbly. He didn't get far into the hall. Instead, as a beggar should, he sat by a pillar near the door, and waited to be noticed.

Telemachos called Eumaios over. He took a whole new loaf from the bread basket, and filled a plate with meat.

'Here,' he said, 'give these to the stranger. No one will go hungry in Ithaka, while I'm here to help them.'

The suitors all saw how well Odysseus was treated. They were furious. Athene made things worse. She put it into Odysseus' head to go round them, one by one, begging for scraps.

Odysseus came to Antinoös.

'Well?' the suitors' leader said, sharply. 'Who are you, and what do you want?'

Before Odysseus could answer, Melanthios the goat-herd broke in.

'Who he is, I don't know. But that fool Eumaios brought him here.'

'Eumaios!' shouted Antinoös. 'I might have guessed! You're a fool, Eumaios. Aren't there enough tramps in Ithaka already? What d'you mean by bringing in another? He'll get nothing from us. You'd better share your own dinner, if you're so anxious for him to be fed.'

Nobody said anything. Odysseus stayed where he was, without moving. Antinoös lost his temper.

'What god has sent this plague to spoil our dinner? Get out of my way, old man! You'll get nothing from me!'

Odysseus answered quietly, 'No, my lord. I see that. A nobleman by birth you may be – but not by manners.'

'What? How dare you insult me?'

Antinoös picked up a wooden stool, and hurled it at Odysseus. It smashed into his shoulder. Odysseus' anger blazed; but once again Athene laid an invisible hand on his shoulder. Without a word, he turned away, and went back to his seat by the pillar.

Telemachos ran to him.

'Sir,' he said, 'I'm sorry to see you treated like this, in my own father's house.'

'Never mind,' said Odysseus, so that everyone could hear. 'If I'd been fighting for my own property, a blow like that would have been fair enough. But Antinoös attacked unfairly. If the god of beggars hears me, I pray to him to punish Antinoös. Let him die, before he ever gets to his wedding day!'

'Sit down, you old fool!' shouted Antinoös. 'If you can't control your tongue, get out of here. Another word, and I'll have you beaten, and thrown into the yard.'

Everyone was surprised by this outburst.

'Antinoös,' called one of the suitors. 'Be careful. Zeus is the god of travellers. He may be watching. Or perhaps this stranger here is one of the gods himself, travelling in disguise. Never insult a stranger. It could be dangerous.'

'Rubbish!' snapped Antinoös. 'A filthy beggar like this – a god? Don't be such fools! Get on with the feast, and forget this tattered old man!'

Grimly, Telemachos went back to his place. The feast went on. But the gods were watching. Only they, and Odysseus, knew what was in store for Antinoös, before the day was done.

The pressure mounts

Next, another beggar came into the palace. His name was Iros. He was a big, tough-looking man. But he was lazy, and a coward. No one had ever seen him working. He'd been a beggar in Ithaka as long as anyone could remember.

He saw Odysseus, sitting by the pillar. He went over, and jostled him with his foot.

'Get up, old man! That's my pillar. Clear off, or I'll beat you up!'

Odysseus didn't move.

'Be careful,' he said quietly. 'The gods are watching. They'll decide who does the beating up, and who gets beaten.'

'Big talk!' sneered Iros. 'Stand up, and fight. You'll be sorry, I warn you.'

Antinoös saw what was going on.

'Look!' he shouted to the suitors. 'Two ragged crows fighting for scraps! Let's make them box for their dinner.'

The suitors roared with delight. A circle was cleared in the middle of the hall. The suitors began making bets with each other. Antinoös called to Iros and Odysseus.

'Here,' he said. 'The winner will get free food for life. The loser will be thrown out, for the dogs to chase.'

Odysseus stood up straight.

'All right,' he said. 'I'm old, but I haven't forgotten how to fight.'

He hitched up his cloak, and bared his arms. They were strong and muscular. Iros panicked.

'Not so fast!' he whined. 'Can't you take a joke? There's plenty of food for two. No need to fight.'

'Oh yes there is,' said Antinoös. He grabbed Iros' cloak, and pushed him into the open space in front of Odysseus.

Odysseus wondered what to do. Should he really hurt Iros, and get him safely out of the palace? Or should he just deal with him gently so that he'd still be there when the killing started?

He made up his mind. Iros came at him half-heartedly. Odysseus sidestepped. As Iros blundered past him, Odysseus chopped his hands down on the back of Iros' neck. Iros fell to the ground, groaning. Blood poured out of his nose and ears. His fingers scrabbled helplessly on the earth floor.

'There,' said Odysseus. 'Now, get out and don't come back.'

He went to his pillar, and sat down. As for Iros, he picked himself up, and slunk out of the palace. He spat blood, and cursed. He didn't know it, but Odysseus had just saved his life. He went up the rocky path in the dark, groaning, to try his luck somewhere else.

Telemachos brought Odysseus a cup of wine.

'Drink up, old man!' he said loudly, so that all the suitors could hear. 'You won, and you can eat free for the rest of your life.'

Odysseus took the cup, and drank.

'Thank you, my lord,' he said, loudly, then added softly in a voice only Telemachos could hear:

'Get ready, son. It won't be long now. The gods are gathering.'

Telemachos went back to his place, and the feasting began again. Odysseus sat quietly by his pillar. As it grew colder, the maids brought iron baskets of blazing logs, and set them up round the hall. Odysseus called them over.

'Go to bed, girls. Stoking fires is man's work. I'll see to it. You go to bed, and keep out of trouble.'

'Trouble?' giggled the prettiest of the girls. She was a silly flirt called Melantho. She had no more brain than a peacock. She fluttered her eyelashes at Odysseus.

'What sort of trouble do you mean, old man?'

'Never mind. Just go to bed.'

'Who are you to order us about? A smelly old beggar from the back streets! I'll do what I like. I'll go to bed when I want to – and with anyone I want, too!'

Odysseus stood up. He didn't need to speak. He towered over the maids. They fled, shrieking with terror. Odysseus went quietly to Telemachos' throne. No one noticed him.

'It's time, Telemachos. Take all the swords and spears, and lock them away. Tell the housekeeper to lock the women's apartments. She must not open the doors till morning, whatever she hears.'

'Yes, father.'

Telemachos went and told the housekeeper what to do. Then he and Odysseus began collecting all the weapons from the hall, and locking them away. Athene helped. She covered them with an invisible mist, so that the suitors wouldn't notice what was happening.

Telemachos saw that as he and Odysseus worked, a beautiful golden light went with them. Athene was like a pillar of sunshine in the dark hall.

'Father,' he whispered, 'what is it? What's causing it?'

'Shh!' answered Odysseus. 'The gods are helping us. The last hours of my exile have come.'

As soon as all the weapons were hidden away, Athene went to Penelope. She didn't appear to her, but whispered in her ear. Penelope thought it was a dream. But she knew she must do as she was told.

She went from her apartments to the store-room. Inside was King Odysseus' treasure. There was gold and silver, bronze and iron. His weapons were there too – the hunting-spears, the war-spears, and the huge bow and quiver of deadly arrows that no one else had ever handled.

Penelope unlocked the door. It had been shut for so long, that the leather hinge growled like a bull, complaining to itself in a green water meadow. The gods heard the noise, and thought to themselves, It's beginning.

Penelope went into the store-room. Standing on tip-toe, she lifted the huge bow from its peg. Her slaves brought the quiver, full of shining arrows. There were twelve axes, too – huge, double-headed axes. Each one had a five-centimetre hole at the top, where the hafts[1] joined the heads.

Carrying the bow, Penelope went down to the suitors in the hall. Her slaves followed. She propped the bow against a pillar, and stood silently beside it.

Silence fell. Every eye was turned her way. She knew that the final struggle was beginning. She knew the words she had to say. Athene had taught her well.

'My lords, it's time. Time to end this silliness once and for all. Tonight I'm going to choose my husband.'

There was an excited buzz. When it stopped, Penelope went on.

'There are twelve axes here. Telemachos is going to set them up in a row. Then the contest will begin. First you must string the bow. Then you must shoot one arrow through all twelve axeheads. The man who wins tonight will be my husband.'

The suitors looked at one another. They'd all heard of Odysseus' bow. Each of them wondered if he'd be the lucky man. None of

[1]haft: handle.

them knew that the gods had already decided who would win.

Telemachos stood up, and swung his cloak clear of his shoulders. At his side hung a sharp sword. He jumped down, and dug a long trench in the earthen floor. He planted the twelve axes in the trench, so that the eye-holes were in a straight line. He trampled the earth flat, and made sure everything was firmly fixed.

When the axes were ready, he took the bow in one hand, and the string in the other. He looped one end of the string round the bottom end of the bow. Then he tried to bend the bow, far enough to slip the other end of the string over it.

Three times he tried. Three times he did not make it. The bow jerked upright, and the string fell slack.

'Ah well,' he said at last. 'The bow's too much for me. Perhaps I'm too young. Well, sirs, this is your chance. Who wants to try first? Whoever strings the bow, and shoots a straight arrow, will be my mother's husband.'

There was silence in the hall. The suitors looked at one another. Who was going to be first. Who was willing to risk the final test?

The bow

After a long silence, Antinoös stood up.

'Gentlemen, nobody wants to go first. I suggest this plan. Let's go round from left to right, each man trying when his turn comes. That way will be fair to everyone.'

All the suitors agreed that this was a good idea. The only man to look unhappy was Leodes – the one who would have to go first. He sat glowering in his chair, and refused to move.

'Are you afraid, Leodes?' mocked Antinoös. 'Are you afraid to try, in case you lose?'

'Of course I'm not afraid,' said Leodes, getting up sulkily, and picking up the bow. He turned it all round, looking it over. He gave it a few trial twists. Then he threw it down crossly.

'It's no use! What chance have I got? What chance have any of us got? None of us can do it. Penelope's tricked us. No one will be able to string it.'

'What rubbish!' shouted the goat-herd Melanthios. 'All it needs is greasing, to make it supple. It's dried up, from hanging too long in the store-room. Let me see to it!'

He sent a slave to fetch a lump of tallow from the store-room. When it came, he warmed it, and worked it into the wood of the bow. Soon it was greased and shining.

'There. Now the contest is fair.'

One by one, the suitors got up, and tried to string the bow. The bow passed from hand to hand round the circle, from left to right.

Odysseus waited until all eyes were on the contest. Then he slipped out of the hall into the courtyard. Eumaios and the cowherd Philoitios followed him.

In the dark courtyard, Odysseus wondered what to do. Was it time to tell them who he really was? He decided to test them first, to see how loyal they were.

'Eumaios, and you too, Philoitios, tell me, what did you think of those men in there? Suppose Odysseus came home suddenly? If it came to a fight, whose side would you be on – his or the suitors'?'

'Old man,' said the cowherd, spitting into the dust, 'that's what I think of that scum in there. If only the gods *would* bring Odysseus home! You'd soon see whose side we were on.'

Eumaios' eyes flashed in the darkness.

'If Odysseus appeared tomorrow, I'd fight on his side – even against an army.'

'Good. Look, then. Here I am.'

'What d'you mean, here you are?'

'I'm Odysseus – home, after twenty years away.'

'*You*, Odysseus? You're an old beggarman. How can we believe that you're Odysseus?'

'Look at this. You remember the scar I got years ago, hunting? A wild boar gashed my leg. This is that scar. Twenty centimetres long. No man could fake *that*.'

He pulled his rags aside, and showed them the scar. Athene cleared their minds, and they knew that he was Odysseus. Weeping for joy, they seized his hands, and shook them and kissed them.

Odysseus saw that they were loyal servants. He knew he could trust them.

'Let's go back in, now,' he said. 'I'm going to ask them to let me try the bow.'

'They'll never agree to that.'

'No. But whatever they say, you must bring it and give it to me, Eumaios. While I'm stringing it, make sure the women and slaves

135

get clear of the hall. Philoitios, your job is to lock the palace gates. Fasten them, so that no one can escape. When that's done, collect a sword and a sharp spear, and wait in the shadows of the hall, until I give the signal.'

When he'd told Eumaios and Philoitios what to do, Odysseus went back into the great hall. Eumaios followed him in. Philoitios went to lock the gates.

Inside the hall, the suitors were still working on the bow. It had reached Eury-machos by now. He was shifting it about in the glow of a fire basket, trying to warm it till it bent. But that didn't make it any easier to string. Twice Eurymachos bent it down, and twice it snapped straight again just as he was about to string it.

'Damnation!' he said furiously. 'There's only one of us left now. Antinoös. Suppose he can't string it either? What will people say? None of us could do it. None of us was as good a man as Odysseus.'

Odysseus stood up, and went into the light of a fire.

'Gentlemen,' he said, 'you've all seen me. I'm a poor, weak beggar. But once I was a king and a famous archer. Let me try the bow, to see if I've any skill left. Perhaps Apollo, god of archers, will help me.'

'Help *you*?' sneered Antinoös. 'To Hell with you, old man! Haven't you had enough out of us already? Get back to your scraps, and leave the bow to your betters.'

'Eumaios, bring me the bow,' said Odysseus quietly.

There was a howl of anger from the suitors. Eumaios went to pick up the bow. But Antinoös got there first.

'If you lay a finger on it, Eumaios, I'll kill you where you stand.'

Eumaios hesitated. But Telemachos jumped up.

'Antinoös, sit down!' he snapped. 'Who told you you could give orders in my palace? Eumaios, take that bow to our guest, or I'll have you whipped.'

Everyone was surprised at the tone of command in Telemachos' voice. Unwillingly, Antinoös sat down. Eumaios picked up the bow, and took it over to Odysseus.

Odysseus took the bow. The swineherd slipped away through the shadows, to give the servants their orders. Philoitios took up his position, on guard at the hall door.

Odysseus turned the great bow this way and that. He was checking to see that it had come to no harm. The suitors looked at each other, and laughed.

'Look at him! A real expert! Perhaps he collects them. Or perhaps he runs a bow-factory. It's a good thing he's learnt *something* on his travels. He's not completely good for nothing!'

In the middle of all their talk, Odysseus said nothing. He balanced the bow, and gave it a last inspection.

Then, as easily as a musician fits a new string on a lyre, he bent the great bow and strung it. He plucked the taut string, and the bow gave out a deep, low hum, like bees in summer.

That was the second sign. At once, from the clear night sky, Zeus sent a rumble of thunder, and a single flash of lightning. For a second, the great hall was filled with an eerie light. The suitors' faces were pale, and sweating.

Odysseus took no notice. Carefully, he chose an arrow from the quiver. He set it to the string, and drew it back to his ear, until the arrow was at full stretch. Then, without getting up from his stool, he fired, straight ahead.

Not one single axe was missed. The arrow passed cleanly through all twelve heads. As it went, it hissed, like an indrawn sigh.

Odysseus stood up.

'Telemachos,' he said, 'the stranger in your palace hasn't disgraced you. I strung the bow, and shot truly. My skill is still with me. The suitors were wrong. I'm still the man I was. Come here, and stand beside me.'

Telemachos went over. He pushed his cloak aside, so that his sword was ready at hand. In his right hand, he held a tall war-spear. The bronze head gleamed in the fire-light.

'Now,' said Odysseus, 'the time has come. First, these gentlemen must eat the feast they've earned. After the feast will come the dancing. Now it's time for the feast to start!'

The feasting and the dancing

Odysseus' first arrow had gone through the axes. The second was aimed at Antinoös.

Antinoös was lifting a drinking-cup to his lips. It was a big, two-handled cup, made of gold. It was halfway to his lips, when Odysseus' arrow hit his throat. He dropped the cup, and collapsed. The blood gushed from his neck, like wine from the cup. The bread and meat on the table slopped in the mess.

The suitors leapt to their feet. They were furious.

'That was a mistake, old man! You killed a man – now you must die, too!'

Odysseus looked scornfully at them.

'Don't threaten me,' he said. 'You never thought I'd come back from Troy. You infested my palace, insulted my son, pestered my wife. Now I *am* back, and you're going to pay the price. I'm Odysseus, Champion of Greeks, Sacker of Cities, the Lord and King of Ithaka – the man who'll kill you all!'

Eurymachos looked round at the others.

'My friends, you heard him. Are we going to die like cattle, without doing anything to stop him? No! We'll fight – fight for our lives!'

He drew his sword, and went for Odysseus. But Odysseus sent an arrow to meet him. It smashed through his armour, sliced into his nipple and tore his liver open. He fell. His feet danced the jig of death on the dusty floor.

Amphinomos began creeping up on Odysseus from behind. He was just about to leap on him. But Telemachos hurled his spear, just in time. Amphinomos died. His eyes were covered in darkness.

Telemachos ran to Odysseus.

'Father, we must get more spears from the armoury. The fools mean to stand and fight.'

'Run, then, and get them, while I've still got arrows left to shoot.'

Telemachos ran to the store-room. He fetched four shields, four helmets, and eight long spears – the kind that cast a shadow of death when they fly. He armed Eumaios and Philoitios, then went back to Odysseus.

Odysseus had begun with sixteen arrows in his quiver. He'd used the first for the axes, and the next two on Antinoös and Eurymachos. That left thirteen. Thirteen more suitors were unlucky. Each of them died, with an arrow drinking his blood.

Odysseus laid the bow aside, and armed himself with the weapons Telemachos had brought. Then the four of them, Odysseus, Telemachos, Eumaios and Philoitios, stood in a tight circle. The rest of the suitors prowled round them, looking for an opening. They were like hunting-dogs with a family of trapped lions. Each one wants the glory of killing them, but none of them dares to attack first.

While all this was going on, Melanthios the goat-herd had a good idea. He had seen Telemachos opening the store-room, and knew how the bolt was worked. He slipped outside when no one was looking. A few minutes later, he came back with his arms full of weapons. He began arming the suitors.

Soon the ring of men round Odysseus was armed, and meant business.

Melanthios went to fetch more weapons. But this time Eumaios saw him. With a word to Odysseus, he went after him, smashing his way through the ring of suitors. Philoitios went too.

Melanthios was creeping along so carefully,

he didn't see them coming. They grabbed him by the hair, and hurled him to the ground.

'Help! Mercy! I didn't mean any harm!'

'Mercy? There's no such thing for traitors!'

They tied his hands and feet, and slung a noose round his neck. Then they hauled it up over a rafter. Melanthios kicked for a while, but he was dancing the jig of death, and soon grew still.

Eumaios and Philoitios hurried back to the others. They found that a stranger had joined Odysseus and Telemachos. It was Mentor. Odysseus looked into the deep, dark eyes, and his heart pounded.

'Telemachos, the gods are helping us. Athene has come to fight for us!'

'Good. We're outnumbered six to one. Look out!'

He ducked. Six of the suitors had hurled their spears at the same time. But Athene raised a hand, and the spears hung still in the air. Then they dropped, and stuck in the ground in front of Odysseus.

'Quickly! Pick them up, and use them!'

Five hands grabbed five spears, and hurled them back at the suitors. Five suitors died, and their eyes were covered in darkness.

The rest of the suitors drew back. Their

eyes were white – with terror.

There was a flash of blinding light. Athene had turned into a swallow. She darted up, and perched on a rafter. She could see the whole fight from there.

Another spear-cast from the four. This time only two suitors died. The other spears missed. Seeing this, the rest of the suitors gathered their courage, and began advancing. Twenty-six men moved against four.

But Athene was watching. She lifted one wing. There was another flash of lightning, and a peal of thunder. Terror and Panic – the slaves of War – overcame the suitors. They stampeded through the hall, like runaway cattle.

Odysseus and his men went after them. Shields cracked, chests caved in, hearts burst. The floor was covered with blood and corpses. The air was thick with groaning.

Odysseus cornered Leodes. Leodes fell on his knees, and held out his hand to beg for mercy.

'No, Odysseus! Spare me! I never agreed with the others. I tried to stop them. Don't kill me! Please, Odysseus, please!'

Odysseus looked at him with disgust.

'You were as bad as the rest. Now you're even afraid to die like a man. I won't spare you, Leodes.'

His thirsty sword bit Leodes' neck. Leodes' head hit the floor. The whine in his throat flew away for ever.

The minstrel Phemios was the next to beg for mercy. He had no weapons – just a lyre of tortoise-shell. He knelt before Odysseus, and prayed for mercy. 'Spare me, my lord! I wasn't one of them. All I did was play for them whenever they asked. I'm a man of peace, not war.'

'Get up. You're safe. Go outside the hall, and wait for dawn.'

Phemios left, eagerly. Odysseus looked round, to see who was next to die.

But there was no one left. All the suitors were dead. They lay in heaps on the dusty floor. When fishermen land a catch of fish, they dump them on the dry sand. The fish gasp and wriggle, till the hot sun ends their lives. That's what the suitors looked like, dead in the palace hall.

Odysseus went to Telemachos.

'My son, please fetch the housekeeper out here. There's cleaning-up to be done.'

Telemachos went for the housekeeper. She came fearfully over to Odysseus, picking her way through the blood and corpses.

'Get hold of all the sluts among the maids –

those who slept with the suitors, or gave them any favours. They must come in here, and clean up. They must wash the corpses, so that their families can bury them. The tables are to be scrubbed, and fresh sand sprinkled on the floor. When that's done, send the maids to the courtyard. I'll be waiting.'

Trembling, the housekeeper went to do as he ordered.

While the terrified maids cleared up inside the hall, Odysseus and Telemachos went into the courtyard. They took a long ship's rope. They strung it loosely between two high posts, like a washing line. Then they sat down and waited.

It was nearly dawn when the maids came out. They were terrified. They wept and screamed. There was no giggling at Odysseus this time.

Odysseus made them stand in a line. He placed a noose of rope round each neck. Then he and Telemachos pulled it tight.

The maids flapped about, like washing on a line. They were like doves or thrushes, caught in a net. For a while their feet jerked in the dance of death – but not for very long.

That was the end of the feasting and dancing. Odysseus had returned. His vengeance was complete.

Odysseus and Penelope

When the dance of death was finished, Odysseus and Telemachos went back into the dark hall. Everywhere had been washed clean. But the stink of fear and death was still in the air.

Odysseus called to the housekeeper.

'Bring me a fire-basket, and some sulphur. We must fumigate[1] the house. I want the smell of the suitors out of my nose for ever. When that's done, the others can come in.'

The old housekeeper fetched fire and sulphur. Odysseus fumigated the great hall, the other rooms of the palace, and the courtyard. Soon, nothing was left to remind anyone that the suitors had ever existed.

When it was all done, the housekeeper opened the doors. All of Odysseus' loyal servants flocked round him. They flung their arms round his neck, kissed him and shook hands.

The old housekeeper left them to it.

[1]fumigate: to smoke out germs and bad smells.

147

Chuckling to herself, she hurried to Penelope's apartments.

'Mistress!' she called. 'Wake up! He's home at last. Odysseus is back! All the suitors are dead!'

Penelope's heart leapt. She ran to the housekeeper, and clung to her.

'Dear nurse,' she said, 'is it true? Is it really Odysseus? Are *all* the suitors dead?'

'Every one. We saw nothing. We were locked away safely. But we heard the clang of weapons, and the groans of dying men. Odysseus has purified the palace, and made it fit for a king again.'

'How can you tell it's Odysseus? Someone has killed the suitors, and that's good. But how do you know it's my husband? It may be another stranger, another trick.'

'Come down, and see for yourself.'

Penelope dressed and went down. Telemachos and the servants were in the great hall. Standing beside them was a tall, elderly man with grey hair. He was dressed in beggar's rags. It was the beggar Penelope had seen before, the one who'd dealt with Iros.

Penelope sat down on the queen's throne, and waited. She said nothing. Gradually everyone else stopped talking, too. All eyes were on her and Odysseus.

Telemachos broke the silence.

'Mother! What are you thinking of? Don't you recognise Odysseus? My father? Your own husband, home after twenty years? He's killed the suitors, and made himself King of Ithaka again.'

'Maybe,' said Penelope, standing up, and going to Odysseus. 'Sir,' she said, 'thank you for ridding us of those suitors. You claim you're Odysseus. I don't recognise you, after twenty years apart. But it's no one's business but ours. Send everyone away, so that we can talk alone.'

'Of course, Penelope,' said Odysseus.

He turned to the others. 'We have to be very careful,' he said. 'Don't forget, we've just killed all the leading young men in Ithaka. Every noble family has lost a son or a brother. They'll be after our blood. We must keep them from finding out, while we make our plans.'

As she listened, Penelope felt sure it really was Odysseus who was speaking. No one else was so clever at planning. The servants listened, too. They took in every word.

'Wash yourselves, and put on your best clothes. Then, while Phemios plays for you, dance and sing for the rest of the night. It's nearly dawn now. There are a few hours left before everyone starts to stir. When they hear dancing and singing from here, they'll think nothing has happened. That will give us the time we need. Hurry!'

Quickly they did as he told them. They washed, and put on their best clothes. Phemios began to play. Soon the hall was full of the noise of a feast. The sounds of dancing and singing filled the air.

The early risers, outside, shook their heads at the din from Odysseus' palace.

'Still at it!' they said. 'Another all-night party! Whatever are young people coming to?' And they went on their way. No one guessed what had really happened.

While this was going on, Odysseus went for a bath. The slaves washed him, and rubbed his skin with scented oil. He dressed in a new tunic and cloak, and a new pair of sandals. Athene sent Beauty down from heaven. She poured her spirit over him. He looked taller, younger, more handsome. It was like the final polish a craftsman puts on a magnificent statue.

When he was ready, Odysseus went down to the hall again, and sat down beside Penelope. He called the housekeeper over.

'Well,' he said loudly. 'My wife is a strange one! She still won't recognise me! You'd better make up a bed for me on the porch outside.'

This was his way of testing Penelope.

'No!' she said. 'Take Odysseus' own bed out of our bedroom, and make it up in the corridor outside. Odysseus made it himself, and this stranger will be honoured to sleep in it.'

That was a trick. It was her way of testing Odysseus.

He burst out laughing.

'Move my bed? You're mad, Penelope! I made that bed myself. I know its secret. When I built the palace, there was a huge olive-tree just where the bedroom was to go. I used the tree as a living pillar. I didn't chop it down. I built the bedroom round it. It supports the whole bed. No one could move that bed, without pulling the whole palace down!'

At last Penelope knew it was Odysseus. He'd passed the test. The gods lifted the blindness from her eyes.

Odysseus looked at his wife, and his heart melted with love. They rushed into each other's arms, and hugged and kissed. They they went together to the high bedroom, the one with the pillar of living olive-wood. They undressed, and lay down on the polished bed.

So that they'd have time for each other, before the day began, Athene held back the chariot of the Sun. Fretting and impatient, his horses pawed the clouds. They wanted to be on their way, galloping across the sky, and bringing daylight to men. But Athene wouldn't let them move until the time was right.

In the hall down below, the dancing and singing at last came to an end. Telemachos ordered an end to the feast. The servants went back to bed. Eumaios and Philoitios left the palace, to go back to their flocks. When everyone had gone, Telemachos stretched, and went to his own room, in another part of the palace.

How it ended

While everyone in Ithaka slept, the ghosts of the suitors crowded down into the Underworld. They squeaked and fluttered, like bats in a dark cave. They clustered by the gates of Hell. Hermes, the shepherd of souls, guided them, like a flock of sheep. There was no blood or warmth left in them. They were the dead leaves of men.

Up in the sky, Zeus was watching. He called Athene to him.

'All those ghosts! So many suitors dead! Every family in Ithaka will want Odysseus' blood.'

'When they hear what happened, yes.'

'This fighting must end, Athene. You must see to it.'

'They'll meet to fight today, when the sun is up. I'll be there, and I'll put an end to it.'

'Good. Twenty years is long enough. To a god, it's nothing. But to a man, it's nearly half a lifetime. Give them happiness for a change, instead of war.'

Athene hurried to do as Zeus had ordered. She freed the Sun's horses, and let them gallop across the sky. Daylight came back to men.

Athene appeared to Odysseus. He was asleep in his own bed, beside Penelope.

'Odysseus, get up! There's no time to lose! Collect your men, and leave the town. The people will soon hear how the suitors died. Keep out of their way, until I tell you.'

She vanished. Odysseus got up. He put on a tunic and cloak, and fastened on his sandals. He slung a sharp sword over his shoulder, and took a spear in his other hand. Then he went to wake Telemachos and the others.

'Get up! Quickly! We must be out of the town by the time the sun is hot.'

They all got up, and dressed. They took their shining weapons, and went to meet Odysseus in the courtyard.

Quickly, Odysseus opened the palace gates. No one was about. Like darting rays of light, they ran through the deserted streets. The sun glittered on their weapons. No one saw them.

Soon they were clear of the town. On each side were fields and meadows, well looked after. They belonged to Odysseus' father, Laertes. He was old, but strong. When Odysseus left for Troy, he had retired to his farms in the country. He was tired of palace life.

Odysseus sent the others ahead. He told them to get a meal ready. He gave them his weapons. Then he walked down through the rows of green vines, to meet his father.

Laertes was hoeing. His back was bent, and a hat with a broad brim protected his head from the sun. He looked up when he heard Odysseus' footsteps.

'Who are you, stranger? What d'you want from me?'

Odysseus said nothing. He just stood there. Athene took the darkness from Laertes' eyes. He recognised his son. He ran to him, and held him in his arms.

'The gods are kind, after all! They've brought you back! They saw the suitors' wickedness, and punished them. O Odysseus, how I've longed to see you safely home!'

'Come in now, father. Telemachos and the others are here.'

'But the suitors –'

'They're dead. Every one of them.'

'What about their families? Won't they want revenge?'

'Yes, and we must plan what to do. Come inside.'

They went to Laertes' house. Inside, Telemachos had prepared a meal. Odysseus and Laertes sat down. The slaves placed polished tables beside them. On them were plates of meat and fruit, with bread in wicker baskets. The steward served them wine in golden cups.

They ate. As they ate, they began to make their plans.

Meanwhile, back in the town, word of the suitors' deaths had got about. Weeping and wailing filled the town. Every noble family had lost a son. As they collected the bodies for burial, an angry murmur grew, strong as a forest fire.

'Odysseus is home. He's murdered all our fine young men.'

'Revenge is what we demand.'

'Kill Odysseus!'

'Blood for blood!'

'Revenge!'

The leader was Eupeithes, the father of Antinoös. He called all the people together.

'My friends,' he shouted, 'where is Odysseus? For twenty years he forgets us. Then he comes home. In one night he kills all our young men. Then he vanishes. Blood for blood – that's what I demand. Will you fight on my side, or his?'

There was a roar of support from the suitors' families. They were like their dead sons – cowards on their own, brave in a pack. They all supported Eupeithes. They rushed for their weapons. Then they met again in the town square. Eupeithes took command.

Up in heaven, Athene went to Zeus.

'Now, father?'

'Yes, now. The young men deserved to die. Eupeithes is a fool. He's in the wrong, and he mustn't cause more deaths. Go down, and end the bloodshed.'

Athene flashed down from heaven to earth, like a bolt of lightning. She found two armies facing each other. On one side were Eupeithes and his gang. On the other, Odysseus, Laertes and their men. They'd left Laertes' farm, and come back to town, to fight.

The two groups faced each other in the dust. The sun was hot overhead.

Odysseus and Telemachos were arguing.

'The first blow's mine, this time.'

'Nonsense! Vengeance is mine, and I must end it.'

'Father, let me prove my courage.'

'No. Not this time.'

Athene went to Laertes. She was disguised

as Mentor.

'Laertes, your son and grandson are quarrelling over bloodshed. Don't let either of them strike the first blow. Strike it yourself, and end this business!'

Laertes looked into her deep, dark eyes. Strength flowed back into his old limbs. He raised his spear, and hurled it with all his might.

Eupeithes was just shouting to his men to attack, when the spear hit him. It smashed the cheek-guard of his helmet, and sliced into his brain. Eupeithes fell, and darkness covered his eyes. His useless armour clattered on the dusty ground.

His men gave a roar of fury. They surged forward, like a river in flood. Odysseus and his men braced themselves. They were outnumbered, but they meant to die bravely.

Suddenly, there was a crash of thunder in the clear blue sky. The horses reared in panic. Athene appeared overhead. There was no disguise this time. She was revealed in her full majesty, as a proud, immortal goddess. The men covered their eyes, dazzled.

'Ithakans!' Athene said.

Her voice boomed and echoed round them. Everyone stood still.

'Ithakans, go home! No more bloodshed! The battle is over!'

Like one man, the followers of Eupeithes turned, and fled. Odysseus shouted.

'Now, my men! After them!'

He ran forward. But Athene raised her hand, and a thunderbolt opened the ground at his feet.

'No, Odysseus, Lord of Greeks, Sacker of Cities, Son of Laertes, King of Ithaka! The suitors did wrong, and you punished them. But these people are your loyal subjects. It's not right for them to die.'

Odysseus laid his weapons down. Athene was right. A king should protect his people, not kill them.

But what about those people? Were they still out for his blood? He looked at the knot of relatives.

They were standing like sheep looking for a shepherd. Eupeithes had stirred their anger. Now that he was dead, there was no fight in them. They knew the suitors had done wrong. Their punishment had been fair.

But they had no leader. No one knew what to do next.

At last Laertes showed them. He knelt at Odysseus' feet, and honoured him as King of

Ithaka.

One by one, the rest of them came up, and knelt at their king's feet. He raised them up, and greeted them kindly, one by one.

Odysseus' wars were ended. His long journey was over at last.

The gods had brought him home.